LAFAYETTE

MURDER + MAYHEM

LAFAYETTE

MURDER + MAYHEM

W.C. MADDEN

THE History PRESS

Published by The History Press
Charleston, SC 29403
www.historypress.net

First published 2010

Manufactured in the United States

ISBN 978.1.59629.899.6

Library of Congress CIP data applied for.

Notice: The information in this book is true and complete to the best of our knowledge. It is offered without guarantee on the part of the author or The History Press. The author and The History Press disclaim all liability in connection with the use of this book.

Contents

Acknowledgements

Behind every good writer is a good wife or significant other. I bounce my stories off my wife, Janice, who lets me know right away if I'm on the right track or if I made some kind of error. Without her, I feel lost. She also helps me with editing and research.

I'd like to thank all of those people who gave me interviews or loaned me photos for the stories in this book. Their comments and quotes help to reinforce the information recorded. A special thanks to the Historic Five Points Fire Station Museum for giving me a photo and valuable information for this book. The Tippecanoe Historical Society was of great help in letting me use a crime scene photo and providing me with many files for reference. The Tippecanoe Public Library was also of great help with its microfiche newspaper file and books about the area. And thanks to the staff in the Tippecanoe County Courthouse Records Section for digging up the court records they could find.

I had to deal with several police departments during the writing of this book. My award for the fastest responding police department for mug shots goes to the Mesquite Police Department in Nevada. I called the department and asked for a photo of Steven Farrell, and staff responded within minutes with an e-mail and the photo attached. The Indiana Department of Corrections was also fast and responded with an e-mail and photos attached. Also quick to respond to my requests were the Monticello Police Department and Tippecanoe sheriff's department. The White County sheriff's department had to be reminded that mug shots were a matter of public record, and it responded quickly. The slowest response came from the Lafayette Police Department for mug shots, but Captain Steven L. Hartman personally took care of the matter and came through with the photos before the deadline.

I'd like to acknowledge the Lafayette Police Department more for its cooperation, but I can't because it wouldn't cooperate. The department refused any interviews and requests for a tour or a ride-along. It also wouldn't provide any murder statistics, but the Tippecanoe sheriff's department came through in that department. Perhaps the Lafayette force should be renamed the Lafayette Secret Police? In any case, I did what I could without its input.

INTRODUCTION

In the history of Lafayette and the surrounding counties, a lot of murders have occurred over the years. No attempt was made to write about all of them—just some of the most interesting ones. This doesn't include the one about a farmer who killed a fellow farmer in rural Tippecanoe County in a dispute over a piece of land in the late 1800s. The murderer only received a sentence of five years in jail. That's not much for a murder.

The book does cover the five murders that led to a death sentence in Tippecanoe County. Three were hanged, and the other two were given the needle. The county has averaged four murders per year since 1988.

The book also contains a lot of mayhem, but not every incident is covered—only the ones I thought would be the most interesting. The attempted bombing of the Tippecanoe County Courthouse on August 2, 1993, was not written about, as nobody was killed, the courthouse is still standing and the case was never solved. Speaking of cases never solved, there are several murder cases in the county that haven't been cracked, except for one recent find. The Tippecanoe sheriff's department recently solved the murder of William Cooke in 1980. Police thought that the evidence was lost, but they found it and tested a cigarette butt for DNA; it came up with a match, Dion Watkins, a Texas prison inmate.

In the early days of Lafayette, the town lacked a formal police force and had a small merchant police team of a few men who patrolled the downtown business district at night to prevent burglaries and provide some sort of law enforcement starting in 1825.

Lafayette created a formal police department on August 9, 1853. They were called "Watchmen," or police officers, and given the authority to arrest persons violating city laws or laws of the state. They were authorized and empowered to enter any dwelling in which any felon was harbored. The first elected town marshal was Thomas Jefferson Chissom, and he served two terms before being elected to county sheriff. He was the sheriff who was responsible for hanging three men on the courthouse square after they were tried.

The first police chief in Lafayette didn't arrive until Alfred Cook was appointed in 1867. Then in 1893, the police department was reorganized, and the Metropolitan Board of Police Commissioners ran the department. During the past century, it went through other changes. By 1938, the department had 35 officers and a civilian clerk. Today, the department has 128 sworn officers and 31 civilians.

Tippecanoe County started with one sheriff, and now the sheriff's department has forty-five officers involved in the enforcement division, twenty-one in the jail division and fourteen others in other departments. The department has a Special Response Team, Explosive Ordnance Disposal Team, Water Rescue Team and K-9 teams.

PART I

TIPPECANOE COUNTY

THE THREE HANGINGS IN LAFAYETTE

On January 8, 1855, the Rose Warehouse on the corner of First and South Streets burned to the ground. After the fire, the remains of a body were discovered, and investigators figured that it was the owner, John Rose.

Five months later, on May 3, Cephas Fahrenbaugh was shot and killed in his home near Wildcat Creek. There was no connection between the two murders then, but there would be later.

Within twenty-four hours, Sheriff Jeff Chisom of Tippecanoe County captured the four men involved in the Fahrenbaugh murder case. Two of the men, David Clark and Thomas Longley, turned state's evidence in return for life sentences instead of the death penalty. Their testimonies helped give Abram Rice and Timothy Driskill the death sentence. Rice, a tinner by trade, was twenty-seven years old and was born in Corydon. Driskill was born in Harrisburg, Pennsylvania, and was just twenty-three years of age.

Clark and Longley gave officials the story of what happened. Rice had pretended to be a cripple, and the other men acted as good Samaritans in finding him. They took him to Fahrenbaugh's home to gain entry with this ruse. It worked until Longley pulled a pistol out of his belt. Fahrenbaugh swung at the nearby Clark and knocked off his hat. Longley fired and hit the young man, who staggered outside through the door. Fahrenbaugh fell at the feet of Driskill and grasped his leg. Driskill then picked up a piece of wood and finished him off.

The three hangings were held on the grounds of the Tippecanoe County Courthouse, built in 1845, as shown in this postcard.

A posse caught Clark and Longley after a chase through a wheat field near Wildcat Bridge. Driskill was found in a house of ill repute in the lower part of town. Clark's hat and a knife with the initials "T.D." (Timothy Driskill) were found at the scene of the murder.

Driskill and Rice got the death sentence for their roles in the crime.

Not long after the trial, Clark and Longley told officials that David Stocking was the murderer of John Rose back in January. Stocking had an alibi, but that witness was afraid of the prosecuting attorney and wouldn't testify on Stocking's behalf. The result was his conviction of first-degree murder and a death sentence. The fifty-year-old man was born in New York.

The sheriff decided to hang all three men on a cold January day in 1856. On that eleventh day of January, the men were readied for the gallows erected on the northwest corner of the courthouse square. Before the three were taken to the scaffold, they said farewell to the other prisoners. "Well gentlemen, I reckon there was never a willinger soul to die than I am," said Rice, according to the *Lafayette Morning Journal*.

A large crowd started gathering outside the iron fence hours before the scheduled afternoon hanging. At 2:00 p.m., the bells of the courthouse and churches were tolled to announce the hour of the execution. That brought about a reaction from the people in the crowd, yelling and cursing. A rumor going around the crowd was that the governor had commuted the death sentences of Rice and Driskill and had given them life sentences.

The crowd became unruly and made an attempt to tear down the fence. Some threw stones and other missiles at police officers, who responded by arresting some of the offenders and hauling them off to jail. Twelve men were later fined for their crimes.

Sheriff Chisom paraded the men out to the gallows. After getting them up to the platform, he asked them if they had any last words. According to the *Lafayette Morning Journal*, Stocking stepped forward and said:

> *I have no confession to make. I am not guilty of the crime for which I am about to die, as I could have satisfied the public had I been allowed a new trial. I had no knowledge of the murder until after it was committed. I don't think the testimony of Longley and Clark was sufficient to convict me. Their object was to save themselves by sacrificing me. I cheerfully give up my life. As my last words, I solemnly swear that I never murdered man, woman or child, so help me God.*

According to the *Lafayette Morning Journal*, Rice said:

> *Gentlemen, my name is Abram Rice; you all know me. I came here in 1840. I am now going to die. I die for men who were cowards. I was at Fahrenbaughs' on the night of the murder. I'll tell you about it. Longley and Clark came to me the day before and asked me to buy them some powder and shot. They said they were going to the ice house, where there was a whore, and as some other fellows might be there they wanted to be prepared. Clark went with me and we bought five cents worth of powder and ball. I afterwards met Longley and Clark at Haggerty's. I asked them where they were going. They said to the ice house and asked me to go along. We met Driskill at the swing bridge. It was raining and he had an umbrella. We all went to the ice house. The rest went in, but I was too drunk to climb the ladder. I laid down at the corner of the house and went to sleep. They waked me when they came down and said they were going out to the Wild Cat. They said there were women there. Driskill wanted to take me back home, but I insisted on going along. When we got to the other side of wide water, Longley proposed to change coats, and said if I would act the cripple that he would have no difficulty in getting in. I agreed. We went up to the house and knocked. Farhrenbaugh, I suppose it was, got up and opened it. The boys force* [sic] *me in. There was a low fire. I sat down in a chair by it. Had no sooner done so than I heard a pistol. It appeared to be behind my back, next to the door. It was all over in less than a minute. We started to go out. I asked the boys what it all meant, but got no answer. This gentlemen is the whole truth. I am going to die. I am no coward, but I die innocent of ether murder or robbery. I forgive my enemies and hope that God Almighty will forgive them. I forgive them and leave my love to all.*

Then Rice requested that a stool on which he was sitting be removed. When it wasn't removed immediately, he removed it himself. Then he kneeled and said that he had seen men hanged this way.

According to the *Lafayette Journal & Courier*, Driskill said to him, "Abe, are you going to kneel?"

"Yes," Rice replied.

Driskill then turned to Stocking and asked, "Stock, which way is the easiest to die—kneel or stand? I want to die the easiest way."

Stocking replied that he should stand unless he thought there was a danger of the rope breaking. The sheriff assured them there was no danger of that happening.

Stocking stood, while the others kneeled as hoods were placed over their heads. At 2:22 p.m., the bolt was withdrawn, and the three men were sent to their deaths.

It was the first and last time criminals were hanged in Lafayette.

TEMPERANCE MOVEMENT BEGINS IN LAFAYETTE

The temperance movement was the first social movement to crusade against the use of alcoholic beverages in Lafayette. The earliest signs of the movement came in 1855 during a march in the city.

On June 12, 1855, people against alcohol marched. They carried posters and signs. One group had a sign that read "Love, Purity and Fidelity."

The ladies of Lafayette started a temperance league. In March 1874, they visited saloons. Some saloons wouldn't let them in the door. They would say prayers as a group and also made efforts to stop beer drinking at the county fair.

Temperance organizations played a key part in bringing about the ratification of the Eighteenth Amendment and the banning of alcohol. Prohibition in Indiana began at 11:00 p.m. on February 1, 1918. The passage of the law forced eighty-three bars, two breweries, five bottling works and three wholesale liquor houses to close their doors in Lafayette. About three hundred workers were put out of work. Some bars became restaurants, while others simply closed and became something entirely different.

The Thieme & Wagner Brewing Company, which had been around for sixty years, continued to operate its brewing machinery in the manufacture of "Ye Tavern," a new beverage that complied with the law as to its alcoholic content.

The legal businesses were quickly replaced by illegal businesses. Some places became speakeasies. A speakeasy was called such because bartenders would tell patrons to be quiet and "speak easy" for fear of officials from the Bureau of Prohibition, which was run by the federal government.

Some houseboats along the Wabash River served as speakeasies or distilleries. If they got wind of a raid, they would simply unhook the boat and float down the river to get away. Others were disguised as legitimate businesses. Illegal booze was a lucrative business, which is why some businesses took the chance.

Federal prohibition officers raided some places and arrested fourteen in October 1925, according to the *Tippecanoe County Democrat.* The sites included the Haywood Restaurant, "Dad" Smith's business at Third and South Streets and Charles Yundt's place on North Third Street. Alcohol and white mule, a name for corn liquor, was secured.

On August 12, 1929, the Lafayette Fire Department fought a fire at 2610 Union Street and uncovered a huge distillery. The front of the building had been camouflaged as a private home. The Lafayette Police Department arrested owner Robert J. Horst, alias "Orlando Jack" Horton, on August 29. He never got to trial, as he was executed in gang style.

The Kabbe Building was built in 1887 and was the site for a speakeasy at 1002½ Main Street. Evidence of it was found when it was renovated. Main Street Mercantile now occupies the building. *Photo by author.*

A couple days later, on the thirty-first, the feds made their largest raid on Lafayette speakeasies. The "Sponge Squad," as the *Lafayette Journal & Courier* called them, closed seventeen establishments and arrested twenty people. The raids began at 4:30 p.m. and lasted an hour. Teams of four agents each were used. The places raided included the Rose Delicatessen at 1628 Main Street (the Cole Group now occupies the building). Also arrested were Edna Hicks and Edward Weir at 1002½ Main Street, now the Main Street Mercantile. "When we were renovating an apartment upstairs, we discovered a stash of old beer bottles behind a false panel in the wall," said owner Vanessa Pegan.

Other speakeasies busted in the raid were Bert E. Anthony Billiards at 211 South Street, now a parking lot; 207 South Street, now a parking lot; 22 North Fifth Street, now a parking garage; and 408 South Fifth Street, now an apartment complex.

A large crowd gathered at the county jail at Fourth and Alabama Streets. For the first time in history, court was held there to allow the accused to give bail. All were released after each gave a $2,000 bail.

In November 1931, the feds opened an office in Lafayette because it was "one of the wettest in Indiana," according to an article in the *Lafayette Journal & Courier*.

This empty building at 701 Wabash Avenue was once the Edgar C. Carman Grocers, a speakeasy that was busted. *Photo by author.*

The Lafayette Brewing Company was granted a brewing permit on April 1, 1933. The company on Main Street still exists today. *Photo by author.*

Nearly a year later, an army of federal prohibition enforcement officers led by Mayor Howard Long of South Bend, deputy prohibition administrator for northern Indiana, made a series of spectacular raids on a dozen speakeasies in Lafayette and the vicinity.

The raid came on a Friday night, August 5, and twenty-three people were arrested for running the illegal establishments. The next day a twenty-fourth arrest was made when William Haffner surrendered himself to authorities. Authorities also arrested the owner of a service station in Americus.

In Lafayette, raids were made at the Gray's Restaurant, 1220 North Street; Lason's Place at the corner of Rossville Road and Earl Avenue; Doran's Restaurant, 209 Columbia Street, now a parking garage; the Wabash Hotel, 1119 Ferry Street, now an apartment building; a place located at 1625 East Main Street, now Bar Berry Liquors; Edgar C. Carmen Grocers, 701 Wabash Avenue, now vacant; and Charles R. Hayes Soft Drinks, 514 Salem Street, now a laundromat. The Bend Inn in West Lafayette was hit, as was a place in Battle Ground.

Besides the arrests, the feds took the liquor found, furniture, guns, slot machines and even a pearl-studded gold-inlaid roulette wheel.

As Prohibition came to an end, the Lafayette Brewing Company was granted a brewing permit on April 1, 1933. Legal beer came to Lafayette restaurants on April 7.

Prohibition finally reached an end on December 5, 1933, with the ratification of the Twenty-first Amendment, which repealed the Eighteenth Amendment.

Modern efforts to reduce alcohol-related accidents include the lowering of the blood-alcohol level to .08 when driving.

TRAIN ACCIDENT KILLS THIRTY-FIVE

Halloween 1864 was a tragic day for some Union soldiers returning from the Civil War. They got involved in a terrible train wreck not far from Lafayette.

This large monument at Greenbush Cemetery carries the names of the Civil War soldiers lost in the train wreck on Dead Man's Curve. *Photo by author.*

The mishap occurred about eight miles south of Lafayette on what is now known as Dead Man's Curve. A sixteen-car cattle train was coming south from Chicago. On the same track, coming north from Indianapolis, was an eleven-car passenger train carrying about five hundred Union soldiers going home on leave. We will never know exactly why these two trains collided on the curve. Some say it was because one train was late; others say it was the fault of a new time schedule. Neither of the trains had a flagman at the curve, as was the required rule.

Whatever the cause, it was too late to avoid the crash by the time the engineers saw the other train. Many were injured and thirty-five were killed. Doctors from Lafayette offered medical help, and farmers in the area offered assistance and provided rides into the city.

Most of the dead Union soldiers were buried at Greenbush Cemetery in Lafayette. Their names are inscribed on a large monument, and the soldiers are buried in a row of stones marked "Unknown."

Other train accidents around Lafayette have taken lives. Three African Americans were killed in a train wreck near West Point, south of Lafayette, in 1897.

Plenty of train accidents have occurred directly in Lafayette, as well. Ten were killed in a train wreck outside the Union Depot at Second and South Streets in 1893. Several people lost their lives to trains when they crossed tracks improperly, too.

THE GUILLOTINE SUICIDE

One of the strangest and most talked-about suicides in Lafayette history is the case of James A. Moon.

The farmer from nearby Wea Plains, twelve miles south of Lafayette, had decided to do himself in. He tried chloroform twice, but each time Lafayette police officers revived him. Then the ingenious man decided on something more foolproof.

He loaded up the materials for his contraption and checked into the Lahr House—later called the Lahr Hotel—in downtown Lafayette on the corner of Fifth and Main Streets on the morning of June 12, 1876. He told the clerk that he wanted a room for a week. He had a rather large trunk, so the two-hundred-pound man elicited the help of a bellhop.

After he checked in, he went and had a shave. Then he met with some former veterans with whom he had fought in the Civil War.

Later that afternoon, he started putting together his device. His hammering disturbed his neighbors, so the manager came to ask what all the commotion was all about. Moon told him that he was putting together an invention. He had a huge axe fastened to a hinge device on the floor. He suspended it with a cord to a hook fastened low on the windowsill. He also put together a box into which his head would fall.

The Lahr Apartment building was once the Lahr House, a hotel, at which John Moon committed suicide with a homemade guillotine. *Photo by author.*

He placed himself beneath the axe and stuffed a cotton ball saturated with chloroform inside the box next to his head. A candle on the windowsill slowly burned through the cord and sent the axe down on his neck. It worked just fine. The next morning, his body was discovered.

The manager retained the guillotine device to display to hotel visitors, and it made the Lahr Hotel a popular tourist stop. The hotel, which was started in 1848, went out of business in the 1950s. Mark Twain was once a visitor, as well as President Ulysses S. Grant. And John Purdue made it his home for a while. Now it is an apartment building.

Apparently, suicide must have run in Moon's family. His son committed suicide in Kansas in 1900, and his daughter did herself in at a Chicago apartment a year later.

THE WILD FOURTH OF JULY

Accidents are common every July Fourth due to fireworks and whatnot, but the centennial celebration in Lafayette was especially dangerous and deadly.

The day began with an accident that nearly took a life. A squad of men was going to fire one hundred cannon shots during the day to celebrate the one hundred years of this nation's life. In the morning, thirty-six shots were fired in the midst of a rainfall. At noon, the gun was again manned, and firing commenced for a second series of rounds. Charlie Felix, a well-known painter in Lafayette, stepped up to the rammer and started doing the work himself. As he was swabbing out the gun, a premature explosion took place. Felix's arm was blown to bits!

Captain Sparks, who was in charge of the squad, saved Felix from being killed, because he dragged the man from the muzzle of the cannon just before it blew up. Sparks was scorched by the gunpowder and covered with blood from the victim. Felix was taken to his residence, where surgeons amputated the arm near the shoulder.

Also on that day, a hot-air balloon was launched in downtown Lafayette. The balloon was marked with large characters in the name of W.S. Lingle, the editor of the *Lafayette Weekly Courier.* As the balloon started to rise, John W. Short took his place on the trapeze, which hung below the balloon. Free from its ropes, the balloon went toward the courthouse and struck the corner, causing it to tear and the hot air to escape. The balloon rose to about two hundred feet before it began a rapid descent.

Five thousand people gazed in suspense as it fell to the earth on Sixth Street between Main and Ferry Streets. The twenty-six-year-old pilot was caught under the chin by a telegraph wire and hurled to the alley at the rear of the Second Presbyterian Church. Later, doctors amputated his right leg between the knee and the thigh as the leg had sustained a compound fracture.

Later during the sweltering day, Lafayette police officers had to break up several fights among those who had drunk too much alcohol.

The day was concluded with a murder at Preiss' Saloon. Giles Washburn got into a fight with several men and was beaten to death. Witnesses put the blame on owner Henry Preiss, Antone Hopp and Franz Bonner.

PRIZEFIGHTING WAS COMMON IN 1800S

Back in the 1800s, prizefighting was not an unusual event, although it was illegal and frowned upon because people would bet on the sport and severe injuries could occur.

The matches were usually held out in the country in a barn or suitable arena. They were announced through the grapevine and not the media, as the activity was against the law.

One prizefighter from Lafayette was Richard Keating. He was quite the boxer and fought a lot in the late 1800s. He was backed by Bill Demerly and John Manly of Lafayette.

In one match in 1888, Keating faced a man by the name of Ed B. White of Peoria. They fought in a cornfield in Fountain County, about fourteen miles south of Danville on a Sunday. They were stripped to the waist and entered the ring at 10:00 a.m. Both men took a beating, as they used bare knuckles. By the fifth round, they were both bloodied and bruised. Both had landed illegal punches, but the referee refused to take any action. When White went down in the fifth and failed to get up, the contest was ended.

Because the fight was held on a Sunday (the Sabbath), the *Lafayette Weekly Courier* editorialized against the sport. "Athletic sports and tests of physical strength are legitimate and commendable, as wrestling, but prize fighting is not recognized as lawful and is but a test of brute force and endurance. Let's have no more of it," the newspaper commented at the end of the article.

Back then it was illegal to do a lot of things on the Sabbath, including playing cricket or baseball. You also couldn't pitch coins. And, of course, some stores were closed on Sundays, a tradition that lingers on today.

REVEREND POISONS WIFE

One of the Ten Commandments in the Bible reads "Thou Shall Not Kill." Reverends are all too familiar with those commandments, but there was one in the history of Tippecanoe County who ignored that biblical law.

In 1889, Fred Pettit was the reverend of the Methodist church in Shawnee Mound, about ten miles southwest of Lafayette. He was married to Hattie. Both were originally from New York, him from Mexico and her from White Plains. He graduated from the academy in West Monroe, New York, and taught school. In 1881, he married Hattie Sperry, and they moved to South Bend and had a daughter named Adine. He taught school there and afterward was employed by the Studebaker wagon works. He entered the ministry and was given a small Methodist church at Shawnee Mound. The village was once a rendezvous for Indian warriors. On the summit of the mound, sentinels were constantly on the lookout for white men or other hostile tribes.

Reverend Pettit became a freemason in Lafayette and elevated himself to grand prelate of the command of the Knights Templar of Indiana. He was

Reverend Fred Pettit wore a beard, like many men in the 1800s. *Courtesy of the* Lafayette Weekly Courier.

also secretary of the Battle Ground Camp Meeting Association in connection with other ministerial duties.

In July 1889, Hattie took sick for several days and then died on the seventeenth in the parsonage. Her body was taken to her birthplace in New York to be buried.

People began to talk about the death, and some thought that she was murdered by her husband because he had taken an interest in one of his parishioners, Mrs. Elma C. Whitehead. A grand jury was convened at the Tippecanoe Courthouse in December, and forty witnesses were examined, but no indictment was forthcoming. There was no evidence, just suspicion. An autopsy had not been performed.

Prosecuting attorney George P. Haywood ordered a chemical analysis of Hattie. Her body was exhumed in New York, and Dr. W.H. Peters found traces of strychnine poison in her stomach.

In early December, warrants were issued for the reverend and Mrs. Whitehead. He was arrested in Columbus, Ohio, where he had moved. Both were brought back to Lafayette, and each was given a bail of $10,000. She made bail but he did not. A grand jury was convened on December 20 and produced an indictment charging both with murder.

In March, Pettit asked for a writ of habeas corpus—relief from unlawful detention—but he lost that battle and was remanded. The state then decided to drop the charges against Mrs. Whitehead.

Pettit demanded a change of venue, and Judge Langdon sent the case to Crawfordsville for trial. Pettit found the best lawyers in the area. The trial began on October 8, 1890 in the Montgomery County seat.

Probably one of the most damning testimonies came from a witness who heard Hattie say, "Fred, this tea is so bitter." Soon after that statement, she took ill. A physician also testified that he had examined her and that she

Mrs. Hattie Pettit had curly hair. *Courtesy of the* Lafayette Weekly Courier.

was suffering from convulsions, a symptom of poisoning. The doctor gave Pettit some medicine to give to his wife, but she got worse each time he administered it. He probably added more poison to it. In any case, she died in horrible agony. This gave the prosecution more proof that he had given her some poison in addition to what was found in her system later, according to an article in the *Lafayette Weekly Courier*.

Pettit was found guilty of murder and sentenced to life imprisonment. He was sent to the state prison in Michigan City on January 13, 1891.

While in prison, he proclaimed his innocence. He had his lawyers

Shawnee Mound Farms is all that is left of the town of Shawnee Mound, which was located nearby. *Photo by author.*

file an appeal. In October three years later, his appeal for a new trial was finally granted. When he received word of it on October 20, he was on his deathbed. He told Reverend Father Blackmar of Michigan City, "I have had good news, but it has come too late." He died later that day from consumption (tuberculosis).

The village of Shawnee Mound has since disappeared from the map, and the memory of the murder has faded into history with it.

LYNCH MOB NEARLY HANGS DOUBLE MURDERER

A hanging nearly occurred in Lafayette's early history involving a double murderer.

On November 3, 1890, George Bennett was drinking heavily. As he walked down the street from the drinking establishment, he was confronted by John Workoff. The two probably got into an argument because Bennett was a scab painter and had been blackballed by the railroad union. Bennett ended the argument by pulling out his pistol and shooting Workoff in the gut on Fifth Street near the *Lafayette Journal* office.

Bennett then escaped the scene down an alley. When he got to Ferry Street, William H. Scott saw him with pistol in hand and asked him what he was doing. Bennett let his gun do the talking and shot Scott twice, killing him almost instantly. Jerry Sheehan then overtook Bennett and held him down until Captain L.C. Clark reached the scene to arrest him.

Workoff was taken to his father's home in serious condition. A doctor was called to help him, but he couldn't save him, and Workoff soon died from the gunshot wound in his abdomen.

A grand jury indicted Bennett for first-degree murder, and the trial was set for May. As the trial date approached, some Lafayette residents became restless and decided to take justice into their own hands. A lynch mob was formed and stormed the jail, but Bennett was nowhere to be found. Sheriff Thomas G. McKee was expecting the visit and had moved Bennett to a secret location.

At the trial, Bennett's lawyers played the insanity card, but the judge and jury didn't see it that way and found him guilty of first-degree murder. He was given a life sentence on June 12 and sent to the state penitentiary at Michigan City. His wife divorced him soon after that.

A new century arrived, and Bennett did go crazy, so prison officials sent him off to Central State Hospital in Indianapolis. In 1908, he escaped the hospital but was soon recaptured and returned. He died at the hospital on January 14, 1910. His body was returned to Lafayette for burial at Spring Vale Cemetery. He was about sixty years old.

THE RUDOLPH RIOT OF 1893

A few riots have occurred in the history of Lafayette, and one in 1893 was dubbed the "Rudolph Riot" by the *Lafayette Morning Journal*.

Professor George P. Rudolph, a Catholic priest in Clyde, Ohio, for a number of years, came to Lafayette to speak on January 26 at the Opera House on behalf of the American Protective Association. The subject of his speech was "Why I left the Romish Church."

He began his lecture by giving some background information about himself. He told the audience that he was born in Switzerland and had Roman parents. His parents were Catholic, and their ambition was to have him enter priesthood. He told about the several schools he attended and the circumstances that led him to immigrate to America.

In the middle of his evening lecture at the Opera House, a number of angry voices came from the recesses of the stage. Then some men appeared on stage with guns, and there was a pistol shot. A man armed with a club rushed toward Rudolph and struck him. The professor fell over a chair, and before he could get to his feet the man struck him again. The professor finally regained his feet and pulled out a pistol. He fired one shot in the air.

Then all hell broke out in the theatre! Women were screaming, men were swearing and others drew weapons ready to shoot. Some chairs were thrown. Blows were struck. Some ran to the front exits to escape the pandemonium. The cry of "Fire!" was heard.

Some men on the stage escaped into the crowd, fearing for their lives now that the professor had the upper hand. They only made the situation worse.

Theatre employees attempted to quiet the audience down, but they were unsuccessful. Sheriff W.A. Gaddis arrived about 9:45 p.m. and tried to restore order with an appeal from the stage. His effort also failed. He then called for volunteers to deputize them and quell the disturbance. Several men responded, and they gathered on stage. That action put an end to the disturbance, and the men didn't have to go into action.

On the advice of the sheriff, Professor Rudolph announced that the completion of his lecture would come at a later date. He denounced the protestors. He said he didn't kill his assailant because he had other engagements and could not remain in Lafayette to attend a trial.

A week later, a grand jury was convened, and indictments were handed down for several people involved in the riot at the Opera House. Three men were arrested and charged with a variety of crimes: assault and battery with intent to commit murder, assault with intent to kill, conspiracy to commit a felony, riot and disturbing a public meeting. Ten others were charged with riot and disturbing a public meeting.

Some fines were later paid, and some went to jail for a short spell. At least nobody was killed in the fray.

POLICE OFFICER DIES MYSTERIOUSLY

In the annals of unsolved murders and deaths in Lafayette, there is one that occurred more than a century ago involving a Lafayette police officer.

When the Big Four Train No. 10 left Lafayette Union Station about 1:00 a.m. on Saturday, September 9, 1893, Officer John Springer was aboard the passenger train. Ahead of him in a car was Officer Coyle. When the train stopped at the Monon crossing, Coyle got off and looked for his fellow officer. He blew his whistle, but there was no reply. Coyle returned to the station, but Springer didn't report for the next train. Coyle became worried and notified Captain Rinard, who went over Springer's beat twice without finding him, so the two officers went down the tracks to search for him.

Carrying lanterns, the officers walked down the tracks slowly, looking for him during the cool evening. They came across his body at 2:35 a.m. Blood was still oozing from a ghastly wound on Springer's head. His scalp was laid wide open and pulled down over his face, the skull being crushed above the right eye, according to an article in the *Lafayette Daily Courier*.

Coroner Davidson decided that Springer must have struck the side of a car in falling, and death was likely instantaneous.

The officer's watch was still running, but the chain was broken. Officials ruled out robbery by a tramp as they found $102.55 in his pockets, as well

The Big Four Train Station as shown in this postcard was a busy place back in 1893 when Officer John Springer lost his life.

as the watch. They thought that the thirty-two-year-old officer might have tried to leap from the car; however, he could also have been pushed. Fellow officer Wicks had been recently pushed from a car platform by a tramp and narrowly escaped serious injury. In any case, the death was ruled accidental.

The funeral was held on Monday at St. Mary's Church. He was survived by his parents, Mr. and Mrs. John Springer of 37 Thompson Street.

He was one of the first metropolitan police officers appointed and was regarded as one of the most efficient men on the force. He was well liked by his fellow officers.

WOMAN FOUND KILLED IN HER HOME

One of the first gruesome murders in Lafayette's history comes from 1895. Police found the body of Mrs. Hester Curtis in her home on December 22. She had been struck in the head four times with a sharp instrument, and blood was splattered on the walls, ceiling and floor. In her hand was a bank account book showing a balance of $488.

Police arrested neighbor Jesse White a few hours later and charged the illiterate man with murder. A few weeks later, White was indicted for the Curtis murder. White was convicted of the murder and given a life sentence.

Two years later, a woman identifying herself as Dora Smith wrote a letter to the Tippecanoe County sheriff. In it she said that three other men had killed Curtis, and she told him where he could find the murder weapon and stolen jewelry belonging to Curtis. Sure enough, the sheriff found the missing jewelry in the hiding place the woman described—but not the murder weapon. However, the three suspects were never found, and White ended up dying in prison on March 14, 1901.

WORST FIRES IN LAFAYETTE HISTORY

Lafayette has had its share of fatal fires over the years, but the worst ones came some time ago.

The deadliest fire in Lafayette's history came in 1906. The members of the Solomon Gaiba family were asleep in their beds on the second floor at 626 South Twenty-second Street when the fire broke out shortly before 11:00 p.m. on July 6 in the summer kitchen. Six children were sleeping in one bedroom, and the parents were asleep in their bedroom.

When the parents discovered the fire, they tried to rescue their children. Mrs. Gaiba went upstairs to wake the children. Apparently in his haste, Solomon fell out the window and was spared the fire. The rest of his family died trying in vain to get out. After the blaze was extinguished by the Lafayette Fire Department, the firemen found the victims. Two captains found a baby's body first on the floor of the front room. At the foot of the bed they found the mother. In the rear bedroom they found four of the children. And downstairs they found the body of a boy. In all, seven died in the fire, according to the *Lafayette Daily Courier*.

The first death of a fireman in the line of duty occurred in 1914. Captain John Mitchell died after fighting a fire at the Dryfus Theatre on April 10. After the fire was put out, the building was deemed hazardous, and Chief Charles Johnson warned his men to stay away from the walls, which could come down at any time. Captain Mitchell was underneath the marquee when a portion of the cornice fell from the top of the building onto the marquee. He attempted to escape but was hit by the falling debris. He sustained internal injuries and died later that day at St. Elizabeth Hospital.

The next deadliest fire occurred on February 8, 1944, at the National Homes Plant. The company was founded in 1940 and built barracks to

People gathered the day after a fire broke out at the home of Samuel Gaiba, at 626 South Twenty-second Street. *Courtesy of the Historic Five Points Fire Station Museum.*

house soldiers. The fire broke out in the paint booth of the plant about 9:30 p.m. By the time the Lafayette Fire Department arrived, the whole plant was ablaze. It was clear from the start that the firefighters were fighting a lost cause. When the smoke cleared, it was discovered that three employees had died in the fire and three were injured. Herman Gilbert, Dallas Ruch and Frank Richardson perished in the blaze.

The Lafayette Fire Department was called to the Wonder Bread garage at 5:20 a.m. on Friday, November 20, 1953, to clean up a gasoline spill. The bumper of a bakery truck had hooked on to a gasoline pump hose, causing gasoline to spill all over the floor. An employee had turned off the electricity, and the fireman and some employees had started cleaning up the smelly mess. As they were in the process of cleaning it up, someone turned on the electricity again. The power caused a pilot light in a gas furnace to jump into the gasoline. The result was an explosion! The blast caused the fuel and flames to cover the men inside the building.

It took the fire department two hours to put out the flames. A dozen men were taken to Home Hospital, some with extensive burns. The building was a complete loss.

At 2:15 p.m., Captain Clarence "Bud" R. Anderson, who was serving as the acting assistant fire chief, lost his life. Four hours later at 6:30 p.m., twenty-six-year-old fireman Walter Leaman Jr., a hoseman, died. The next day, Captain

A dozen men from the Wonder Bread factory fire were taken to Home Hospital, as shown in this postcard.

Marshall J. Leaman, fifty-one, died from his injuries. It was the worst fire in terms of firemen lost and injured in the fire department's history.

Anderson was a seventeen-year veteran of the fire department. The fifty-year-old was born in Lafayette and attended schools there. In 1924, he married Marie Carte and joined the department. He was promoted to lieutenant in January 1952. Then he was promoted to captain in August 1953.

Walter Leaman was the nephew of Captain Marshall Leaman, who also perished. Walter was born in Indianapolis but grew up in Lafayette. He served with the U.S. Army Air Force in World War II. He married Betty Jean Cochran in 1947 and was appointed to the fire department in February 1953, so he had only been with it for nine months.

Captain Leaman had been a member of the fire department for twenty-two years. He had been promoted to lieutenant in 1940 and made captain in 1948.

Four other firefighters and two employees were injured in the blaze.

On November 26, 1965, four girls died and four were injured in a blaze at 2212 Meadow Drive. The fire occurred in the home at 4:00 a.m., and William Jackman was unable to rescue all of his children. He did save two of them before the flames and smoke became too much for him. Four of his daughters died: Donna, sixteen; Connie, sixteen; Deborah, six; and Lisa, three months.

FIRST MURDERESS OF COUNTY STRIKES

The first case with a murderess in Tippecanoe County occurred in 1906. It would not be the last.

Alice Cooper and Charles A. Lawson were married in Lafayette in 1888. Charles was a bartender at a saloon at the corner of Fifth and Columbia Streets. After the couple was married for five years, he opened his own saloon at 428 Columbia Street. The year following the opening, Alice delivered a baby girl. They named her Ethel. The family lived in an apartment above the saloon.

Years passed, and their daughter grew up. In 1905, the couple bought a home at 1109 North Street. While the couple didn't always get along and quarreled often, divorce wasn't considered. They had a child to support, and she was now twelve.

On Friday, September 21, 1906, Alice and Ethel went down to the saloon to get Charles, since he had failed to come home for dinner that evening. He had been on a drunken spree for the last two weeks. They entered through the side door of the saloon. Charles was standing behind the bar about ten feet away from them. Also behind the bar was bartender William Russell. Two men were drinking.

The couple started an argument and called each other names. Charles escalated the argument by throwing a heavy beer glass at his wife. It missed. He then moved around the bar toward her in a threatening way. She pulled from her purse a revolver that she had bought for him and started shooting. The first two shots missed. Then she pulled the trigger three more times, and they hit the mark. As her husband stumbled from the shots, Alice grabbed her daughter and hurriedly left.

Colonel George A. Harrison and Dr. M.S. Hooper were in a nearby drugstore when they heard the shots. They came running to the saloon. Harrison saw Alice coming out with the pistol in her hand. He pinned her arms to her side and took away the pistol. "Let me alone," she cried out.

The colonel followed the doctor into the saloon. Charles was leaning against the cigar case, blood pouring from his chest, shoulder and hand. As the men approached, he fell to the floor. Dr. Hooper removed his own shirt and tried to stop the bleeding.

Meanwhile, the colonel went after Alice, who had wandered away with her daughter. "Oh, Mama, why did you shoot my Papa?" Ethel said, according to the *Lafayette Daily Courier*. The colonel caught up to them and escorted them to the police station, where he had once been the superintendent of the Lafayette Police Department.

Charles Lawson was shot to death by his wife at a saloon at 428 Columbia Street, which is believed to be where Three Blind Mice Antiques is now located. *Photo by the author.*

Superintendent Powell went to the crime scene with some other police officers. He was greeted by a large crowd, so Powell closed the doors to the bar for privacy. An ambulance arrived, and Charles was taken to it by stretcher. The police officers had to fight their way through the crowd to get him to it. The horse-drawn wagon carried the police officers, Dr. Hooper and the prosecutor. Charles died en route to the hospital, so the ambulance was directed to the police station instead.

When officers told her of his demise, Alice refused to believe it at first. After she decided that it was the truth, she was not overcome with grief. Alice refused to describe the shooting but told police that she was justified in doing so. She told them that she didn't know if any of the shots she fired hit Charles.

Police searched her purse and found a box of .32-caliber cartridges for the Smith & Wesson revolver.

Before Alice was taken off to jail, her daughter Ethel was crying hysterically and said, "What will I do if they take you away? Papa is gone and I'll be all alone."

The next day, Alice employed a couple of prominent attorneys, and they told her not to say a word to anyone. A writer from the *Lafayette Daily Courier* speculated that she would probably claim self-defense.

Alice was allowed to attend her husband's funeral. This time, she cried and showed much emotion. After the funeral, she was sent back to jail.

Alice Cooper Lawson's trial was held in June the following year. She was found guilty. Defense attorney Will R. Wood (a senator) tried in vain to get the verdict overturned on a technicality, but it was of no use. Judge DeHart overruled the motion and gave Alice a life sentence. She was sent to the Indiana Women's Prison in Indianapolis.

Alice only served three years in the prison, as she was paroled in October 1910 by Governor Thomas R. Marshall after a recommendation by the state board of pardons. Alice was given a full pardon by Governor Samuel M. Ralston on December 11, 1914.

MAN KILLS LITTLE GIRL HE LOVED

In the history of Lafayette, only a few murders have involved children. The first may have well been the one in 1907.

John Vaughn had worked for some time as a section foreman for the Monon Railroad. Then he worked periodically as a fireman at the ice plant and light plant. However, he was not employed in May 1907. The thirty-six-year-old bachelor lived along the east side of the canal just outside of the Lafayette city limits.

Vaughn had a liking for little girls and wanted eleven-year-old Lizzie Strubel for his wife, but her parents wouldn't have it. So on May 4, he decided to take matters into his own hands. If he couldn't have her, he didn't want anyone else to have her.

He was walking her home along with her fourteen-year-old sister and two brothers when he pulled out his pocketknife and attacked her not far from her home. He began stabbing her in the chest. She screamed in agony. Her brothers and sisters ran home. He stabbed her again and again and again. He stabbed her a dozen times before she died. Then he laid himself on top of her body and turned the knife on himself. He stabbed himself in the neck ten times but failed to hit a major artery.

Her brothers and sisters told her father, and he came running to the scene. He threw Vaughn to the side, picked up his daughter and carried her home.

Police were called, and Officer Kelm responded from the Salem Street Depot. He boarded a switch engine and had the engineer take him near the home. He found Vaughn sitting on a box in the yard and took him into custody.

A patrol wagon took Vaughn to police headquarters, where a curious crowd had gathered. "Lynch him!" someone yelled. Vaughn looked a mess, with blood all over his shirt.

He readily admitted his crime to police and to a *Lafayette Morning Journal* reporter: "When we reached the canal, I realized that Lizzie was lost to me. I loved her and she loved me, but we could never marry on account of the opposition of her parents. When I realized this, a desire came over me to kill her and then to kill myself. I began striking at her with the knife, and after I was satisfied that I killed her, I tried to kill myself."

Vaughn was placed in the jail hospital, and a doctor treated his wounds.

A few days later, a grand jury returned a first-degree murder charge against Vaughn. However, he plea bargained and pleaded guilty to second-degree murder in exchange for life in prison on May 20. His defense would have been insanity had it gone to trial, according to the newspaper.

DRUNK KILLS MAN, GETS LIFE

Back more than one hundred years ago, a murder occurred about seven miles southeast of the city in a place called McCoy Woods.

Two boys were out in the woods on August 16, 1907, hunting for squirrels when they discovered an unconscious man who had been shot just above the right eye. A revolver containing one empty shell was found on the ground about six inches from his head. Also found at the crime scene was a beer bottle. The boys ran to the home of L.J. Hudlow, who with the help of some neighbors carried the man to the nearby home of James Rayburn.

Dr. Reser, who was acting as coroner, was called, as well as Dr. Pyke of Romney. Dr. Pyke probed the wound and determined that the man had not committed suicide—the bullet had passed through his soft brown hat with a large brim in a downward angle, as if the man was dipping his head when shot. Since the man had no identification and a nickel was found at the crime scene, they deducted that robbery may have been the motive. The man's identity was unknown. He was taken to St. Elizabeth Hospital by ambulance, where doctors discovered that he was paralyzed on the left side of his body. He died the next day. The man was finally identified as Clarence H. Summerfield.

The sheriff investigated the matter and found out that the man had been seen with another man in a buggy. Witnesses said that they drove through

St. Elizabeth Hospital, as shown in this postcard, is one of the oldest hospitals in Lafayette and has had its share of treating criminals and police alike. Neal Hockstra would visit the hospital before he committed his double murder-suicide.

Conroe and appeared to be intoxicated. They had stopped at the Rayburn home for a drink of water. Then Mr. Rayburn's son heard a shot but thought that it was someone hunting for squirrels in the woods.

Deputy Sheriff Boyer and Detective Weinhardt arrested Edward Vaughter for the crime, but he was later released after his alibi proved that he wasn't there at the time of the murder. The police then arrested James Whitinger after he was identified by witnesses as the man with Summerfield.

Whitinger's trial lasted only fifteen minutes as he decided to plead guilty to second-degree murder instead of being tried for first-degree murder as the grand jury had recommended. He received a life sentence, which made him eligible for parole after twenty years. The prosecutor admitted that the charge of first-degree murder was not justified because the defendant was drunk at the time and didn't have the mental capacity to realize the nature and consequence of his act, according to a *Lafayette Daily Courier* article.

RICH FARMER KILLS FARMHAND

Nowadays, when someone is arrested and accused of murdering someone, they usually always get remanded to jail until the case is heard. This is done in order to keep the suspect under lock and key so he doesn't flee or do something else. Back a hundred years ago, that wasn't the case in the Conrad Ortman murder trial in Lafayette. The suspect, Ellas Ray, was let out of jail on a $50,000 bond. That was a lot of money back then, but Ray was a rich farmer.

Ray was accused of killing Ortman on the night of May 25, 1909. The two got into a quarrel in the hog lot of Ray's farm. Ray reportedly struck his young farmhand with a stick of stove wood and gave the young lad a brain concussion, from which he later died. Ray was arrested for the murder but got out on the bond.

The farmer owned 2,500 acres of land and carried a large life insurance policy. He was reported to be worth $750,000—a very large sum in those days. Millionaires were rare. He was born in Vermillion County, Illinois, on November 12, 1844, and had lived in Tippecanoe County since he was a baby. His farm was located six miles south of Lafayette.

The trial was scheduled for November. On November 17, Ray asked for a change of venue, but Judge DeHart failed to grant it. According to the *Lafayette Daily Courier*, after the hearing, Ray told his son, Frank B. Ray, "They refused me a fair trial. I would rather be in my grave than in a penitentiary, and a trial."

So instead of facing a trial, Ray killed himself the next day. He stabbed himself in the neck with a pocketknife and then shot himself in the chest with a shotgun. His housekeeper, Elvira Hart, didn't hear the gunshot, although she was in the house at the time of the incident.

The news of the suicide came to the court as the jury was going to be selected. Judge DeHart dismissed the case immediately and wrote the following entry into the record: "On the suggestion of the death of the defendant this case is ordered abated."

One of the most memorable murder cases in the county's history up to that time concluded without a trial.

KKK BEGAN IN LAFAYETTE IN 1923

During the Roaring Twenties, the Ku Klux Klan became very active throughout the United States, including in Lafayette. Founded in 1865 after the Civil War, the Klan or KKK was known for protecting the rights of white Americans through the use of violence and intimidation. Members burned crosses, hanged people and caused havoc across the land.

The Klan first arrived in Lafayette in the early 1920s. Mayor George R. Durgan got wind of a planned march in January 1923 by the white-robed

Klansmen and quickly called a meeting to pass an ordinance making their march illegal. The city council passed an ordinance prohibiting the wearing of masks, except on Halloween night, and fixed a penalty of ten to fifty dollars with costs of prosecution. "The time has come," said the mayor, "when we Protestants and I am one of them, must take a stand for the preservation of law and order in Lafayette. We are a peaceful, law abiding community. Peace and harmony prevails and I believe it is the desire of every good citizen that this condition continue."

Tippecanoe Klan No. 20 flourished and claimed twenty-five thousand members in the Lafayette area. The group burned some crosses. A group of Klanswomen from around the state met in Lafayette on September 3, 1925.

Klan members' influence diminished after Klan leader D.C. Stephenson was convicted of murder in 1925 in Indianapolis. The Klan's popularity fell even further during the Great Depression and World War II. The organization gathered some steam again in the 1950s and 1960s when African Americans fought for civil rights.

In more recent times, the Klan has made some appearances in the area. Sixteen members of the Klan marched in Crawfordsville on July 26, 1986. They obtained a permit to march and carried the U.S. flag, a Confederate flag and a silver coffin to symbolize death to pure races. They were met by counter-demonstrators carrying signs like "Equality for all races" and "Help end racism."

Then in March 1987, a small group of Klan members marched in Delphi to protest the barring of two brothers—Darwin and James McCurdy—from school property. They had been in a fight at a school dance. Their father, James, asked for the Klan's help to protest.

Grand Dragon Ken Taylor said that the march would get media attention, and it did. A group of eleven KKK members marched in downtown Delphi carrying a gray coffin. A group of about two hundred gathered to view the march.

Then on April 2, 1994, a Klan rally was held in Crawfordsville, and about five hundred people attended. The Klan also decided to hold a recruitment rally in Lafayette. Their plans were met with a counter-group, Greater Lafayette Race Unity Coalition. The rally was held on the steps of the Tippecanoe County Courthouse, and riot police were on hand.

A year later in Attica, thirty-six members of the Klan marched in their black-and-white robes. They were invited by some merchants, according to Christopher Johnson, the imperial klaliff of the Knights of the KKK.

PROSECUTOR KILLS RUMRUNNER

Prosecuting attorneys are the lawyers who take criminals to court and try to convict them of a crime. One prosecuting attorney in Lafayette took the law into his own hands and killed a rumrunner in 1923.

Prosecuting attorney Morris R. Parks had written a letter requesting the help of the U.S. attorney general in busting an illegal liquor operation. The attorney general sent Officer Lyle, a prohibition enforcement officer. The African American officer made arrangements to buy illegal alcohol from the suspects. He then informed Parks of the location. Parks got together a team of officers to assist him in the bust on the evening of Thursday, July 19: Sheriff Joseph R. Jackson and his deputies W.C. Campbell and Louis Boelkins.

The four men hid in weeds at the north side of Dayton Road. At 6:30 p.m., two automobiles turned from the brick pavement to Indianapolis Road. The federal team of African Americans, with Lyle and two other officers, was in the first car, a Ford.

In the second car were the bootleggers, Carl B. Stierle and Forest "Humpy" Fay, a pair of African Americans.

As the cars stopped, Parks and the officers hiding in the weeds made their way to the cars as the transaction was taking place. Meanwhile, Lyle pulled out a pistol and told the pair of criminals that they were under arrest. Parks was afraid that they would drive away, so he jumped on the running board of the car. Stierle struck him in the face, breaking his glasses. Parks thought he saw Stierle go for a gun, so he shot twice, and one of the bullets hit the man in the chest, killing him.

Homicides in Tippecanoe County
1988-2009

1988 - 9	1994 - 2	2000 - 2	2006 - 7
1989 - 4	1995 - 5	2001 - 7	2007 - 2
1990 - 4	1996 - 4	2002 - 8	2008 - 7
1991 - 2	1997 - 0	2003 - 2	2009 - 2
1992 - 6	1998 - 3	2004 - 7	Average
1993 - 4	1999 - 2	2005 - 5	per year: 4

Over the last twenty-two years, ninety-four people have been murdered in Tippecanoe County, an average of four per year. *Statistics courtesy of the Tippecanoe Sheriff's Department.*

Sheriff Jackson and Deputy Sheriff Boelkins took Stierle to Home Hospital, where he was declared dead. The other officers looked for the gun that Parks said he saw, but they didn't find one. Fay said that Stierle didn't carry a gun.

The sheriff also confiscated the vehicle and booze for evidence. Later, Sheriff Jackson placed Parks under arrest, since no gun was ever found.

A couple of days later, Stierle was buried in Spring Vale Cemetery. He was born in Lafayette on February 1, 1896, and had lived his entire life in Lafayette. He left behind a wife, Bertha, who had left him and filed for divorce in Indianapolis.

On October 18, a grand jury exonerated Parks of the killing.

POLICE CAPTAIN KILLED IN BANK ROBBERY

During the Roaring Twenties, bank robberies were common throughout the land, including in Lafayette.

On November 1, 1927, a daring gang of robbers held up the Tippecanoe Loan & Trust Company. They were daring because the bank was located across the street from police headquarters.

When the robbers entered the bank, they demanded that the seven employees and one customer go to the rear vault. Margaret Cheney acted quickly and ran into the vault first and set off the alarm.

Captain Charles W. Arman heard the alarm from his office just 150 feet away. He was alone in the headquarters, as two of his men were in court. He ran across the street and into the bank. When he entered the building, Helen Cheney, Margaret's sister, came in right behind him. "I walked into the bank with Captain Arman," Cheney explained afterward to the *Lafayette Journal & Courier*. "He had come running from police headquarters and had reached the bank's door just as I arrived from the post office where I had gone for some registered mail. The captain opened the door and I walked in with him. Then I saw several men standing near the cages with guns drawn. Instantly, I knew that a holdup was going on. I turned to a stairway near the door to run up to the mezzanine."

As she got there, she heard one of the men say, "There you are; we'll get you." Arman pulled out his revolver and the shooting began.

One bullet hit the captain in the face near his nose and entered his brain, killing him instantly. He dropped dead about twenty-five feet from

Helen Cheney returned from the Lafayette Post Office, as shown in this postcard, to discover the bank robbery in progress.

the door. He had wounded one of the bandits with a shot to his neck. The bank robbers dragged their wounded comrade to the awaiting car. Helen came down the stairs and checked on Arman, who was covered in blood. She then looked out the door and saw the robbers in their Hupmobile with Iowa license plates heading north on Fourth Street with highway policemen firing at them. The robbers were last seen heading through Chalmers north to Chicago.

After months of investigation, police arrested two suspects in the case. In June, police arrested Edward Meadows, alias Edward Metcalf, thirty-three, in Hammond. Then they took Louis A. Fields, fifty-five, of Wolcott, into custody. The third suspect, Charles McGray, was already in jail. He was serving a ten- to twenty-year prison sentence in the Michigan City prison for a robbery in Decatur.

On September 25, 1928, Chicago police officers arrested Robert E. Stanley and held him for extradition to Lafayette. Helen Cheney was brought to Chicago by Indiana state policemen. She identified him as one of the five robbers. She also identified another man from police files, Len Liakos.

Two years later, on December 30, 1930, Police Chief John H. Kluth announced that three of the five bandits in the December 16 bank robbery in Clinton were part of the gang that robbed the Tippecanoe Loan & Trust and killed Captain Arman. Officials and clerks in Clinton identified Herman K. Lamm, Walter H. Dietrich and William H. Long as the bandits. They

The bank robbers fled in a Hupmobile, much like the one shown in this postcard.

were also identified by Tippecanoe Loan & Trust workers as the bandits in 1927. One suspect committed suicide in Sidell, Illinois.

On January 5, 1931, Dietrich and Long were convicted after eighteen minutes of jury deliberation and given a life sentence for the Clinton robbery of the Citizens State Bank.

The Fraternal Order of Police in Lafayette named its lodge after the captain—Lafayette Arman Lodge #49.

TWO DEPUTY SHERIFFS KILLED

During the Roaring Twenties, a few Tippecanoe County deputy sheriffs met their fates at the hands of a couple of criminals.

A pair of West Lafayette thieves robbed a West Point restaurant in 1927. Sam Baxter and John Burns were later arrested for the crime and convicted. Judge Homer W. Hennegar sentenced the pair to serve sentences of five to twenty-one years in the state reformatory.

On February 7, 1928, Baxter and Burns were transported by John P. Grove and Wallace McClure, Tippecanoe deputy sheriffs, in a Studebaker touring car. When the car didn't arrive in Michigan City, foul play was suspected.

The mystery was solved nine days later when the bodies of the deputies were found side by side in a farm pasture near Foster in Warren County, a few miles west of Covington. Both deputies had been shot from behind. Their car was found in a garage in Decatur, Illinois.

Baxter and Burns headed south to flee the Midwest. In March, they were arrested in Atoka, Oklahoma, for carrying concealed weapons and given twenty days in jail. The weapons had belonged to the deputies they had slain. Law enforcement officials didn't know that they were wanted by Indiana and let them go after their jail sentence. However, they had used different names. Baxter even had the audacity to use Foster as his last name.

The pair split up, and Burns came back home to Lafayette. He was captured at George Williamson's home, 204 West Thornell Street, early on the morning of May 21. Burns was tried and convicted of first-degree murder in June and given a life sentence in Indiana State Prison.

The hunt for Baxter continued. The Tippecanoe County sheriff's department started sending out pictures and sets of fingerprints to cities and counties all over the country. In all, more than 1,500 envelopes were sent.

The mass mailing finally paid off on August 27, 1931. Police in Albuquerque, New Mexico, arrested Baxter after they shot him in the leg during the capture. The twenty-four-year-old criminal was brought back to Indiana and tried for murder. He blamed Burns for both murders. He said that Burns hit McClure on the head with a tire wrench, knocking him unconscious. Then Burns grabbed his gun. He later shot both in the back.

The Tippecanoe sheriff's department used a Studebaker, much like this one, to transport the prisoners to Michigan City.

The jury convicted Baxter of second-degree murder on January 8, 1932. He was given a life sentence in the state prison in Michigan City, the same place as his accomplice. Baxter went off to prison and left behind a wife and child. Since he had lived under the alias Al Casey, she didn't even know that he was a wanted criminal in New Mexico.

GANGLAND MURDER IN 1930

Lafayette had its share of notorious criminals during the Roaring Twenties, and Prohibition brought about its share of rumrunners. One of those was a criminal by the name of Jack Horton.

Horton served a term in the federal prison at Fort Leavenworth, Kansas, for interstate traffic in stolen cars. After prison, he became active in bootlegging from Chicago to Indianapolis. The thirty-three-year-old had a wife living in Indianapolis, so he spent much of his time running liquor from Chicago in high-powered cars and stopping in Lafayette on his way to Indianapolis. In Lafayette, he operated from a camouflaged building on East Union Street.

Lafayette police officers arrested him for liquor manufacturing in 1929, but the feds took over the case. He was to appear in a U.S. district court for that charge on March 17, 1930. They released him from a Crown Point jail on a $10,000 bond. He also was charged with robbery and a shooting at the Edwin R. Bowles home on 610 Oregon Street in early 1930. Lafayette police officers didn't know why he shot Bowles, although it was suspected that he was under the influence of drugs at the time.

He never ended up being tried for those crimes—his body was found in a strawberry patch four miles southwest of Lafayette on the afternoon of March 5. Wallace D. Miller of West Lafayette found the body on Neal Cadwallader's farm while driving a little-used side road. Horton's body was about thirty feet away from the road lying face down. He notified the Lafayette Police Department. Coroner M.G. Frasch performed the autopsy and found the body riddled with bullets—five .38-caliber in his back. Police suspected that he had been shot elsewhere and that his body was dumped in the field.

Police believed that Horton was killed by some rival gang of bootleggers whose territory he had violated, according to a *Lafayette Journal & Courier* article. He had been known for hijacking enterprises between Chicago and Indianapolis. Horton was a desperate man with many enemies in the business.

The police never found Horton's murderers but figured that he had been killed by other criminals and that maybe someday they would catch them for something else. Back in those days they didn't have the forensic knowledge wielded today.

PATROLMAN SHOT TO DEATH IN ALLEY

One Lafayette patrolman was killed over twenty-three dollars. The year was 1931. Of course, twenty-three dollars back then was a lot more money than it is today, and it happened during the Great Depression, when money meant a lot and many were in short supply of it.

An outlaw robbed the Kenneth Lockard Mid-Continent gas station on North Ellsworth Street in West Lafayette about 8:15 p.m. on August 4. The attendant notified police of the description of the car, a Buick with Illinois plates.

The burglar drove across the Wabash River into Lafayette. His car broke down on Columbia Street, and he took flight at a jog. Meanwhile, Lafayette police captain Albert A. Nichols and Patrolman Harry R. Farrell got into a patrol car to investigate the robbery. Harold W. Vess also heard about the robbery and saw the man running west on Columbia Street, so he jumped onto the running board and pointed out the man to the police officers. The police gave chase.

The man ran to Third Street and turned south. When he reached Alabama, he turned west and went a half-block before turning into an alley, with police in hot pursuit. As they entered the alley, Captain Nichols got out of the patrol car, and Vess jumped off the running board while Farrell continued down the alley. The captain went around the block to head the bandit off.

When the burglar came out of the alley, he spotted the captain cutting off his escape route, so he ran back into the alley. The desperate criminal was cornered. He pulled out his revolver and shot at Farrell. Farrell returned fire. A bullet shattered the right side window of the police car. Then Farrell was hit in his shooting hand. A bullet to his abdomen sent him staggering against his police car, but several of his shots found the criminal's body. The culprit found an opening in the alley fence and stumbled away.

Several people living off the alley heard the shots and came to the policeman's aid. Farrell got into his police car but didn't have the strength to drive away. However, one of the neighbors, Melvin Kallenberger, took Farrell to the hospital, where he died soon after getting there, according to a *Lafayette Journal & Courier* article.

Meanwhile, Captain Nichols started searching the area, not aware that Farrell had been shot fatally. But he was not looking in the right places. Other police officers soon arrived on the scene from the sheriff's office and the state motor police. They found the body of the dead criminal after following his

The Standard Oil Station in downtown Lafayette is reminiscent of the station that was robbed in West Lafayette in 1931. It is the Red Crown Mini-Museum on South Street. It was built in 1927–28. *Photo by author.*

blood trail. It lay by the back door of a nearby home, about two hundred feet from the shooting scene.

By this time, hundreds of people had already gathered near the scene. When they heard that the criminal was dead, they cheered police.

The next day, the criminal was identified by a Chalmers man as Louis E. Jeffries. However, the relatives of Jeffries declared that the corpse at the Soller Funeral Home was not Jeffries. The Buick the criminal had been driving was identified by the gas station attendant as the car driven by the burglar, so the police had that one right.

Meanwhile, a funeral was held for Farrell. He left behind a wife and two children. Farrell was thirty-six. He was born on a farm in Round Grove Township, White County, on January 16, 1895. He attended Otterbein High School for two years. Farrell came to Lafayette three years prior to the fatal shooting. He had been a patrolman for fourteen months.

A few days later, the criminal was identified as Kenneth Harold Stout, a twenty-one-year-old ex-con from Wisconsin. The staff at the U.S. Department of Justice identified the photo and fingerprints sent to them by Lafayette police officers. Stout had spent some time in Wisconsin State Prison for burglary.

CIVILIAN SAVES THE DAY IN POLICE SHOOTING

In 1933, the country was deep into the Great Depression. Jobs were scarce and people were desperate. Gangs roamed the country looting and vandalizing. One gang showed up in Lafayette on Friday, June 16.

Two men, James "Heavy" Richardson and Frank "Slim" Byrd, showed up at the Wabash Valley Sanitarium that day. Byrd had a bone infection. Doctors became suspicious and referred the men to Dr. F.L. Loop at the Lafayette Life Building. The manager of the sanitarium followed the men, while Lafayette police officers were notified of the suspicious men.

Captain Edgar Hill and a squad of four men were sent to the doctor's office to investigate the matter. They arrived about 4:30 p.m. The captain strategically stationed one man by the suspect's vehicle, one at the corner and one at the entrance. He took Patrolman Forest Goldsberry with him up to the second floor. When they opened the door, Richardson stood there with guns drawn. He took the officers' weapons, and then the two gangsters ran down the stairs to escape.

As the criminals came out of the building, they shot Patrolman J. Wesley Wilson in the abdomen. Then they ran to the corner of the Life Building and turned north, firing at officers as they ran. As they rounded the corner, they shot Patrolman James McDonald in the legs. He went down in a heap. Officer Paul Klinker, who had taken position by their auto, ran on to Main

James "Heavy" Richardson and Frank "Slim" Byrd mistakenly went to the Wabash Valley Sanitarium, as shown in this postcard, for medical treatment, as Byrd had a bone infection.

The 1933 gun battle occurred near the old Lafayette Life Building, as shown in this postcard in downtown Lafayette.

Street from around the Third Street corner and fired at the men. They returned fire and hit him in the chest and pelvic area. He went down as well.

Little did they know that Assistant Manager Harry Houston had followed the pair from the Wabash Valley Hospital and witnessed the shootings. Houston picked up Wilson's machine gun and then ran upstairs to the second floor. He climbed out onto the fire escape and mowed down the fleeing suspects, hitting both of them in the abdomen.

Two bystanders were shot during the gun battle. Paul Roby, fourteen, of Chalmers was hit by a stray bullet three blocks away from the scene of the battle. It shattered his ankle. The other was Jack Hopkins, sixteen, a postal telegraph messenger, who was one block away on Fourth Street. He was hit in the ankle, too.

The injured officers were rushed to the local hospital, and the wounded suspects were taken to the police station before being taken to the hospital for treatment.

After the battle, police officers also took Ruth Edgar, nineteen, of Frankfort into custody. She had been waiting in their auto, which had Georgia license plates and was parked on Third Street near Main. In the car they found a rifle, shotgun, several hotel keys and Kentucky license plates. The hotel keys came from the Forbis Hotel in Monticello, the Morton Hotel in Indianapolis and hotels in two other states. A bullet hole was also found on the rear of the vehicle. The Frankfort woman later claimed that she knew nothing of the activities of the pair. She was held as a material witness on a $5,000 bond.

Police also arrested another member of the gang that night. Sheriff W.J. Hayes of White County took Richardson's brother, John, into custody at a cottage near Monticello. He was camping on Lake Freeman with two other men and a woman. Police found several guns in the cottage. He admitted that he was the brother of James.

More than a thousand Lafayette residents gathered near the gun battle and then went to police headquarters, where they remained throughout the night. They also gathered around St. Elizabeth Hospital to get more word about the fallen officers. The *Lafayette Journal & Courier* put out an extra edition of the newspaper and sold four thousand copies in a few hours.

The following day, James Richardson died at 2:00 p.m. from the two wounds in his chest. He was thirty-three. The Nashville, Tennessee native had two aliases: P.T. Murphy and Bob Sanders. His partner, Frank Byrd, was in serious condition with seven gunshot wounds. When Byrd was told about the fate of his partner, he said in a *Lafayette Journal & Courier* article, "There goes the best man that ever breathed."

On Sunday, Patrolman Wilson died of his wounds at St. Elizabeth Hospital. The forty-four-year-old single man had suffered four gunshots to the abdomen. Wilson had been on the force since 1929. He was survived by his mother, Mrs. Naomi Miller of Lafayette. The others involved in the shooting were showing improvement, including the other bandit.

Police officers later discovered that Byrd was an alias and that they had Dudley Richardson in custody, a nephew of the dead bandit. They had been members of an eight-man gang that had performed a double bank robbery in Cullom, Illinois, on June 3 that year.

In October, the murder case against Dudley Richardson was moved to Carroll County after his attorney requested that it be moved because of too much prejudice in Tippecanoe County. The judge agreed and moved the case to Carroll County.

On January 22, 1934, the case against Richardson began in Delphi. The case against him was as solid as the courthouse in which it was held, and Richardson was found guilty of second-degree murder on February 3. He was given a life sentence and shipped off to Indiana State Prison in Michigan City.

MURDER-SUICIDE RUINS CHRISTMAS

World War II had come to an end. Christmas was quickly approaching. Three sons were returning from the army for the holidays. Sounds like a good setting for a joyous time. Such was not the case for one family in Lafayette in 1945.

This crime scene photo was taken in the 1940s. *Courtesy Tippecanoe Historical Association, Lafayette, Indiana.*

December 15 began as a cold day. Clyde Lucas, who lived on Colfax Street, was putting up his Christmas tree and discovered some bulbs out on his string of lights, so he went next door to Neal Hockstra's home to borrow some tree bulbs. He knocked on the door and there was no answer. As he returned to his home, he noticed no smoke coming from the chimney of Neal's home. Clyde became concerned and called the police.

Lieutenant Joseph M. Clark and Detective Sergeant Edward J. Shaw arrived soon after the call and knocked loudly on the front door. No answer. Clark peeked into the windows and saw a body slumped in a chair in the living room. This gave him probable cause to kick in the door.

Inside, the officers found a horrible, cold scene. Neal Hockstra had shot himself in the head, and his cap had been blown off by the blast from the shotgun, which lay between his legs. In the kitchen they found Mrs. Hockstra face-down in her food and coffee. She had been shot in the back of the head. In the bedroom they found the daughter, Edith, still in her bed and also shot in the back of the head.

Coroner John S. Morrison said that it was plainly a case of double murder and suicide, according to the *Lafayette Journal & Courier*. Police theorized that Neal first shot his wife and then his daughter before killing himself.

Neal, a linoleum layer, had suffered a nervous breakdown in September and had been treated at St. Elizabeth Hospital for a week and the Wabash Valley Sanitarium for six weeks. After he returned home, he continually brooded.

Mrs. Hockstra, who was born in Holland, was working at Loeb's department store at the time. The daughter was attending Jefferson High School.

Instead of returning home to celebrate the holidays, the sons returned sadly to attend the funerals of their family members.

POLICE OFFICER COMMITS MURDER-SUICIDE

The history of Lafayette has one murder of which the Lafayette Police Department is not very proud, because it involved one of its own.

On a late August day in 1962, Melvin Felix of Mulberry was driving behind another car on Union Street when he heard gunshots coming from the car in front of him. The car then came to a screeching halt at the south curb of the street, and a woman staggered out of the driver's side.

Melvin went around her and stopped in front of the car. He got out and rushed to her aid. By then, she had fallen to the pavement in misery. He looked inside the car and saw a man slumped over in the seat, blood splattered all over the place. Then Melvin ran to a nearby home to call police.

A couple of neighbors in the 2200 block heard the shots and tires squealing and came running to the scene as well, but there wasn't anything they could do. The man in the car was dead, and the woman was near death.

A few minutes later, the police and an ambulance arrived at the scene. The woman was rushed to St. Elizabeth Hospital. She died on the way. She was none other than Betty Eileen Howe, the wife of Sergeant Orville "Bud" Howe of the Lafayette Police Department. She had been shot while she was driving the car by her husband. Then he had shot himself in the head with his .38-caliber police revolver.

County Coroner Dr. Robert E. Williams examined both bodies and declared it to be a murder-suicide. Police said that the motive was "marital trouble," according to the *Lafayette Journal & Courier.*

The two had been married only two months. He had been previously married, and she had been married twice before.

Bud Howe had lived most of his life in Lafayette. He graduated from Jefferson High School in 1933 and served three years and four months in the navy in the pacific theatre during World War II. He joined the police force on May 15, 1946, and was promoted to sergeant on September 1, 1956. He was a member of the Arman Lodge 49, Fraternal Order of Police, the American Legion, Eagles and Trinity Methodist Church.

He had been in a serious car accident a year before and sustained several severe injuries. His girlfriend, Lillian Rost, died in the crash.

Betty Howe was also a native of Lafayette and owned and operated Jerry's Beauty Shop. She was a member of the Eagles Auxiliary and Veterans of Foreign Wars Ladies Auxiliary in Lebanon.

Exactly why Bud shot his wife only God knows; however, his action certainly left a mark on the history of the Lafayette Police Department.

MISSING PERSON TURNS INTO MURDER

One former Lafayette resident got away with murder for five years before he was arrested and finally put in jail.

Darrell Duane "Duke" Kincaid of Lafayette attained a criminal record in his early twenties, including second-degree burglary, forgery, larceny and contributing to the delinquency of a minor.

He married Marjorie Ann Reuzenaar in Lafayette on February 28, 1966. Their marriage lasted a few years before Darrell got tired of Marjorie and filed for divorce on December 8, 1968. However, the two decided to get back together, and the divorce was dismissed three days later.

A year later, on December 8, Marjorie turned the tables and filed for divorce. This time the divorce went through, in March 1970, but the couple started seeing each other again after the divorce and lived together with their two daughters and one son.

In August 1970, the two got into an argument one night at 1010 South Second Street. "Duke Darrell went over there and I know he hit her," said James Robert Strong in a deposition later. "He started beating on her. I went and tried to pull him off once. He pushed me out of the way and said, 'Get away from me, fella!' and then kept beating her."

Marjorie died from her beating, so Darrell wrapped her in a painting tarp. (Darrell was a painter by trade.) Then the two men took her body to a road in Battle Ground and dumped it six feet from the road. Darrell covered the body with some bags of dirt he had in his truck. He told Strong not to utter a word about this to anybody.

Reuzenaar was reported missing. She had been working at the Traffic Club on Main Street as a waitress. Their son, Joseph, went to live with his grandmother, while his two sisters, Tina and Laurie, moved in with their aunt later on.

Three years later, Kincaid moved from Lafayette to Logansport to work as a carpenter and live. Strong kept his mouth shut.

Five years passed.

On March 22, 1975, a boy found a skull in a dry cistern near Battle Ground, two-tenths of a mile from where Darrell had grown up. The Tippecanoe sheriff's department investigated. Dental records helped the coroner determine that the skeleton was that of Marjorie Ann Reuzenaar. The dentist also found evidence that she had been struck in the mouth prior to death. Her mother, Betty, identified the clothing at the scene as that worn by her daughter. Coroner Dr. Grayson Davis concluded that her death came through violence, according to the *Lafayette Journal & Courier*.

Police arrested Kincaid on April 2 and charged him with the murder. Strong told police about what Kincaid had done, so the case against him was as clear as a pane of freshly cleaned glass.

Kincaid was found guilty of murder and given a life sentence. On July 11, 1975, he was sent to the Indiana penitentiary to serve his sentence.

In April 1977, Kincaid filed a lawsuit against Tippecanoe County and Sheriff John Rusk for violating Sixth Amendment rights. A bench trial ruled in Rusk's favor on June 1, 1978. Kincaid filed an appeal. Rusk died the following year.

The U.S. Court of Appeals found in favor of Kincaid (that his right to reading material had been violated) and awarded him one dollar on February 10, 1982. It was a very small victory for a convicted murderer.

Kincaid also filed a suit against Daniel Eberle of the Indiana State Police for giving false testimony to the grand jury. He got nowhere with that one.

A year away from his release date in 1992, he requested a reduced sentence on September 11, 1991. Judge Ronald E. Melichar denied the request a few weeks later.

He was released one year later.

His son remembers when he got out. "I was shocked," said Joseph, who goes by his mother's maiden name. He still remembers the beatings Darrell used to give his mother and him. He would even tie up his mother. "I remember times when he choked her," he said in an interview. He was only seven years old back then.

Today, Darrell still lives in the Lafayette area, according to his son, who also lives in Lafayette. Joseph said that Darrell's been in trouble with the law, too. And now his father is in his sixties.

Joseph has lost track of his sisters. The murder is one thing in life that he will never forget.

DOUBLE MURDER LEADS TO DEATH SENTENCE

One of the worst Tippecanoe County murders in modern times resulted in the death sentence for one criminal.

To the southwest of Lafayette lies the small town called West Point, established in 1878. Mark and Gertrude Thompson lived in a country home near West Point. Mark had retired from the life of being a lawyer and was once a Tippecanoe County prosecutor. His son, Warren B. Thompson, was a Tippecanoe Circuit Court judge at the time. By the late 1970s, the Thompsons were in their eighties and hired people to help care for them in lieu of going to a nursing home.

During the summer of 1979, they hired James and Barbara Lowery to take care of them. As part of their payment, the Lowerys lived for free in a trailer on the Thompson property. However, the old couple didn't like the work the Lowerys were doing and decided to fire them. The day Mark fired the couple, they refused to go until Mark wrote them a check for $100 in exchange for leaving immediately. The Lowerys went to live in an old school bus at the Raymar Campgrounds outside of Crawfordsville.

In late September, James Lowery discussed a robbery with his friend Jim Bennett, as both needed the money. Lowery suggested his old place of employment at the Thompsons' house. His plan was to visit the home and rob the Thompsons of money and their expensive gun collection. He also would force them to write a check for $9,000. Then they'd kill them and bury them. Bennett went along with the plot; he needed the money.

When the two arrived at the Thompsons' home about dusk on Sunday, September 30, Lowery was armed with a .32-caliber pistol, and Bennett carried a sawed-off shotgun. They decided to break into the housekeeper's trailer first. The new housekeeper, Janet Brown, was sitting in the trailer adjacent to the Thompsons' garage reading a book. She heard the Thompsons' dog barking outside at something. She looked out the window and recognized Jim Lowery. He pushed his way through her door and said, "This is a holdup."

Lowery grabbed her by the nape of the neck and put his gun to her head. Then he forced her to take him into the Thompsons' home. Bennett followed but stayed outside. Lowery forced Brown into the kitchen, where Mark Thompson was standing. Lowery told him that this was a holdup. "You don't want to do this now, Jim," said Mark, according to court records. He responded by shooting the old man in the wrist. The bullet passed through Mark's wrist and into his side.

Then he had Bennett watch over Mark while he sought out his wife, Gertrude, whom he found in the den watching television. She didn't move fast enough for him, so he struck her in the head with his revolver. Blood spurted from her head and she staggered. After he got Gertrude into the kitchen, he had her sit in a chair. Then he shot the elderly woman point blank in the head. He turned the gun on the housekeeper. Janet put up her hands in defense, which slowed the velocity of the bullet enough to stop it from killing her. She fell to the floor and pretended that she was dead. Mark Thompson managed to trip the alarm, setting off a blaring siren on top of the barn that he had installed to notify neighbors when he needed help. Lowery panicked. He went over to Mark and shot him again. Because of the alarm, Lowery and Bennett left quickly, taking the back roads to avoid the police. They returned to the school bus, where Bennett told Lowery's ex-wife that Lowery had shot the Thompsons.

After they left, the housekeeper called police. When police arrived, Gertrude was already dead and Mark was barely alive. Mark told police that "monkeys" assaulted him. Mark used that term when he forgot someone's name.

Janet Brown was taken to St. Elizabeth Hospital in Lafayette, while Mark was flown to Methodist Hospital in Indianapolis in critical condition. Brown was in stable condition and put under protective guard by police, since she had identified Jim Lowery as one of the assailants. She had met him a week or so before the shooting at the West Point Post Office, where he talked hatefully about the Thompsons.

Lafayette City Court judge Gregory Donat issued a warrant on Monday for the arrest of Lowery and an unnamed accomplice. Police went on an all-out search in the Crawfordsville area for the two criminals. They found them the next day and arrested them for the murder and burglary. Lowery was arrested in a supermarket parking lot in Crawfordsville, while Bennett was arrested at his home. Bennett told officers, "I didn't kill him." Bennett must not have realized that Mark Thompson was still alive.

After his arrest, Lowery made several incriminating statements to police officers. He also told his cellmate of his crimes, describing them in detail.

A few days later, Mark Thompson died from his three gunshot wounds in Indianapolis, so now the two faced double murder charges. Mark's son, Warren, took several months away from the bench to take care of his parents' affairs.

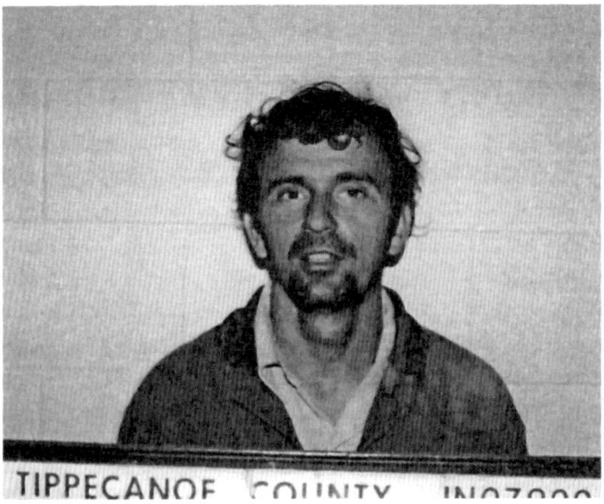

This is how James Lowery looked when he was booked. *Courtesy of the Tippecanoe County Sheriff's Department.*

Lafayette attorney Thomas Brooks was chosen to preside over the case as a special judge. However, the cases against the two were separated and venued to other counties because of all the publicity the case had received in Tippecanoe County. Bennett's case was moved to Howard County, while Lowery's case went to Boone County.

Before Bennett's trial in early June 1980, he was offered a plea bargain. If he were to testify against Lowery, Tippecanoe county prosecutor John Meyers would drop the charges of habitual criminality and not seek the death sentence against Bennett. He would receive a forty-year sentence instead.

The prosecutor had a rock solid case against Lowery with Bennett's testimony, but Lowery refused to plead guilty. Meyers was seeking the death penalty. Before the Lowery trial the same month, his attorney challenged the admissibility of statements he made to a cellmate, and he was successful in excluding only some.

At the trial, Lowery's ex-wife testified against him for immunity from prosecution. Even Lowery's sister, Mary Ann Davis of Darlington, testified against him. She said that he had admitted to her that he killed the Thompsons during one of her jail visits to him.

On June 30, 1980, Howard Circuit Court judge Robert Kinsey changed Bennett's sentencing recommendation and gave him three forty-year sentences. The change didn't make a difference in the time he would serve though, as the sentences were to be served simultaneously instead of consecutively.

Lowery was found guilty, and one month later on July 11 he was given the death sentence. He was the first criminal from Tippecanoe County to get the death sentence in 124 years.

The case was appealed, and on May 5, 1982, the Indiana Court of Appeals overturned the verdict because the jury had not been sequestered.

Another change of venue sent the case to Hendricks County. Bennett, who was serving his term in prison, declined to testify at the second trial. He wanted a better deal from the state, but that didn't happen. When he refused to testify, the judge allowed the reading of his testimony at the first trial to the jury. Lowery tried in desperation to get the death sentence taken off the table. The jury heard about his tough history. Born in 1947 to a fourteen-year-old mother and an alcoholic father, his childhood was marked by poverty and parental neglect. As a teen, he got in trouble with the law, and a judge sent him to a state mental hospital, although he suffered no mental problems. He suffered several gang rapes by the staff at the Norman Beatty Hospital. He was released at eighteen and got involved in drugs, alcohol and crime. Lowery even testified at the sentencing hearing. It did no good. The jury still recommended the death sentence and fifty years for the attempted murder charge.

The case was appealed again, and in 1994 the death sentence was reaffirmed. However, the attempted murder charge was reversed. It didn't matter anyways. He couldn't serve fifty years after death.

This is James Lowery before he was executed for his double murder. *Courtesy of the Indiana Department of Corrections.*

Lowery wrote Warren Thompson, who had retired from the bench in 1984 after twenty-four years as a judge. The letter professed his innocence, according to his wife, Mona. Warren is now suffering memory problems and doesn't recall the letter or the details of the murder.

Lowery tried a writ of habeas corpus in 1996 to seek relief against unlawful detention. The writ was denied by the court in 1999. The writ was appealed, but it was again denied by the Seventh Circuit Court the following year.

Lowery's last-ditch effort to escape the death penalty was a request for clemency from the governor. Governor Frank O'Bannon denied it, according to a *Lafayette Journal & Courier* article.

"Twenty-four jurors and 23 judges have found the death penalty appropriate in this case," O'Bannon wrote. "The process was fair, and I defer to the findings of the courts."

On June 21, 2001, at 12:29 a.m., Lowery was put to death by lethal injection. He was the seventy-ninth convicted murderer executed in Indiana since 1900. His attorneys read to reporters a lengthy note from Lowery after the execution that concluded, "I am so very sorry."

"They were such a loving family," Mona said in an interview about the Thompsons.

GRUESOME MURDER REMEMBERED BY MANY

If you ask people in Lafayette what recent historic murder stands out the most in their minds, most will reply with the 1982 murder by Marcia Heald. The murder was also one of the most gruesome in Lafayette history.

On August 2 of that year, Marcia attended a poetry reading at Gerald and Shelly Smith's apartment at 601½ New York Street. Shelly and Marcia discussed poetry, folk music and antiques that night until after 1:00 a.m. Shelly offered her couch for Marcia to sleep on, but she declined and went to her car instead.

At 5:00 a.m. the next morning, Gerald left his wife Shelly to deliver newspapers. Some time later, Marcia awoke in her car and decided that she had to return to their apartment and kill Shelly because she believed her to be a serpent possessed by Satan.

Marcia first took off all of her clothing in a downstairs bathroom. She also went into the kitchen and grabbed a paring knife. Then she went into Shelly's bedroom. Shelly was lying naked under the covers. She looked like a snake to Marcia, who yelled, "Yahweh's kingdom come" and began stabbing her.

Shelly screamed with pain and ran from the bedroom toward the kitchen, but Marcia grabbed her by the hair, pulled her down and then began stabbing Shelly repeatedly in the head, neck, chest and back. Then Marcia tried to remove the "snake's" head, because she felt that the serpent would rejuvenate if she didn't behead it. She sawed with a knife and part of a mirror. Then she tried twisting Shelly's head off. She gave up in her attempt to remove her head. She went back to the bathroom,

Marcia Heald killed Shelly Smith in the carriage house behind this house, which is now on the National Register of Historic Places. *Photo by author.*

showered, dressed and then left. She drove around for a while and then stopped and ate breakfast at a restaurant near Purdue University.

Later that day, Lafayette police officers apprehended Marcia and got a confession out of the crazed woman.

Marcia was not your typical murderer. The Plainfield resident had been a librarian at the Indiana State Library. The divorced mother of two spent two Saturdays per month at the Indianapolis Children's Museum demonstrating weaving. However, she also told court psychiatrists that she was Eve from the Garden of Eden.

Marcia pleaded innocent by reason of insanity, but the judge ruled that she was competent to stand trial.

Her attorney, Brent Westerfeld, tried to get a continuance before the trial began; he said that his client wasn't competent to stand trial. Psychiatrists differed on whether she was insane or schizophrenic. Two of three determined that she knew what she was doing at the time of the murder.

According to the *Lafayette Journal & Courier*, at the hearing Marcia said, "It was written 2,500 years ago. It would be at Lebanon [where the trial

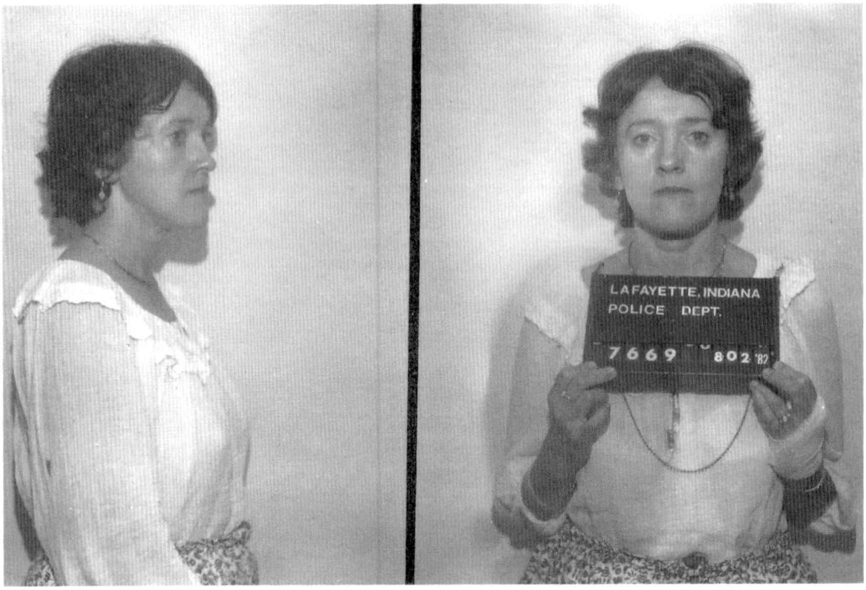

Marcia Heald was booked on August 2, 1982. *Courtesy Lafayette Police Department.*

had been moved to]. It is Yahweh's will. Human beings have no knowledge of my world. They should not meddle. I am not a human being; I am an animal. I became an animal in March."

Her attorney said that Marcia would not get a fair trial with twelve human beings.

Asked who the Messiah was, she replied, "I am. My mission is… to proclaim Christ, to replace religion with Yahweh, to replace law with Yahweh, to replace sanity with Yahweh, to replace death with Yahweh." Marcia added that she had died seven times and had been reincarnated each time. "I'll come back in my next life to finish the mission," she added, according to the *Lafayette Journal & Courier*.

The judge turned down the request for a continuance, and jury selection was made immediately after the hearing. Westerfeld told the jury during his opening statement that his client was trying to kill a snake, not a human being.

During the trial, a coworker of hers, John Selch, testified that Marcia had written down her strange and religious philosophical thoughts. In those writings, she believed that a fellow member (Brian Thornton) of a Lafayette group that did reenactments from the eighteenth century was Christ.

A letter was introduced during the trial that was written the day before Marcia murdered Smith. In the letter, she wrote, "This day Aug. 1 is the last day of my earthly life." That night she killed Smith.

Marcia was the first witness for the defense. She began her testimony by claiming that her name was "Mars, the God of War" and that she was 5,743 years old, though 44 years in her present form.

She later testified, "I began seeing something in front of Shelly [Smith]. I saw this face and I saw it was a snake. Yahweh [God] was sending me messages. I could see something at her neck like scissors or knives. I said to myself, 'Is this the lady I have to battle with.'"

Marcia believed Shelly to be a serpent. "You always have to cut off the head of a serpent," she said.

A jury took only four and a half hours to convict the woman. The forty-four-year-old woman was sentenced to forty years for the murder and thirty years for burglary. She wouldn't be eligible for parole for twenty years. Her lawyers appealed the case on the basis that her Miranda rights were violated, but her retrial was denied.

In 1998, Marcia sought clemency for the murder. She told the Indiana Parole Board that God made her stab and nearly behead Shelly Smith. She said that she felt no remorse for what she had done but that she would not murder again if she were free.

"I think it was a test to see if I would be obedient, and I proved that I was, and the contract is finished," she said during a public hearing. "Yahweh [God] doesn't require me to do that [kill] anymore," she said. "I think Yahweh owes me something this time because of what I did for him."

Needless to say, her request for clemency was denied by the governor.

MURDER CASE OVERTURNED, BUT RESULTS SAME

Not many murder cases get overturned by the Indiana Court of Appeals, but one in Tippecanoe County did.

In 1986, Bryan Brown and David Ohm became friends at Harrison High School in Lafayette during their senior year. Two years later, in October 1988, they met at a Steak 'n Shake in Lafayette to plot the robbery of a retired farmer in Tippecanoe County near Interstate 65.

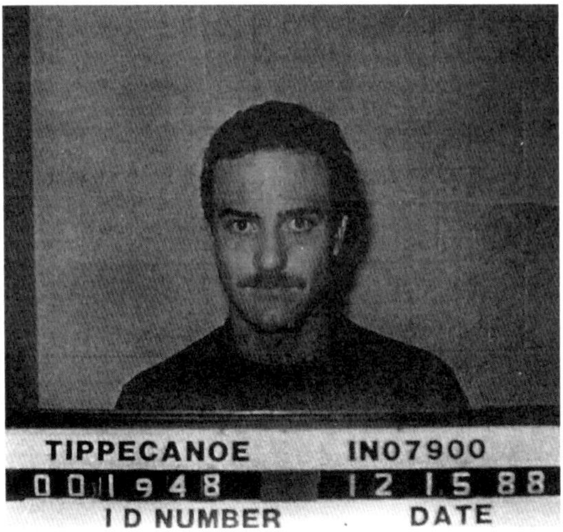

Above: David Ohm had a mustache when he was taken into custody. *Courtesy Tippecanoe County Sheriff's Department.*

Below: Bryan Brown was taken into custody on December 15, 1988. *Courtesy Tippecanoe County Sheriff's Department.*

Brown was mired in debt and needed money to pay off both bills and a drug dealer. He needed his friend to pull off the robbery, because the farmer knew Brown—he had done odd jobs for Lewis H. McKay when he was a teen. He didn't want to be recognized.

At first, Ohm thought that his friend had gone a little crazy and figured that he could talk him out of it. No way. So on October 19, Ohm and Brown went to McKay's home at 9333 North County Road 100 West. Ohm knocked on the door and told McKay that he needed to use his phone. The eighty-year-old man let him in. Ohm saw that McKay was not alone. McKay's friend, John E. Ross, was watching a World Series game on television. Ohm used the phone, thanked McKay and went back outside.

Ohm told Brown of the situation. Brown insisted that Ohm go back, knock on the door again and punch his way in.

Ohm knocked on the door again and McKay answered. Ohm sucker-punched him several times in the face as hard as he could. "Mr. McKay staggered back and fell against the wall," Ohm said in court years later, according to a *Lafayette Journal & Courier* article. "Bryan came in after me and started hitting on Mr. Ross. I saw Bryan beating Mr. Ross half to death. He was holding his arms up. Bryan kept hitting him and hitting him."

Bryan then went to the kitchen and returned with some knives. He gave one to Ohm and told him to kill Ross. Bryan then slit the throat of McKay. Ohm decided he had to do the same with Ross.

The two then went through the house looking for money and treasures. They found $1,200 in cash, some watches, silverware and U.S. Treasury notes.

When the two returned to their car, Ohm became mad at Brown's giddiness over the murders. "He was making jokes about it," Ohm said later.

"Ha, ha, Ohmie, we just got away with our first murders," Brown replied.

The next day, McKay and Ross were found dead by a female friend, who notified police. An anonymous tip led police to Brown, who was arrested in Virginia on October 27. Ohm turned himself in to the Indiana State Police in West Lafayette on November 12.

On August 31, 1989, Ohm pleaded guilty to the murders in an open plea agreement to avoid the death penalty and drop the dozen other felony charges. It took until July 20 the following year before the judge sentenced him to sixty years in jail.

Brown decided to take his chances with a jury, and he ended up getting a lot more time. He was found guilty of two counts of murder, two counts of robbery, two counts of burglary and two counts of confinement. For that he got a sentence of 176 years in prison. However, he did win an appeal of the case in 1992 when the Indiana Supreme Court found the Tippecanoe Circuit Court trial flawed because evidence of a polygraph examination of a witness was improperly admitted.

So, Brown was retried, but it was an exercise in futility by a desperate man—Brown ended up with the same sentence.

JUVENILE KILLS MAN IN HATE CRIME

One death in Lafayette history could be considered a hate crime, and it involved a juvenile. A hate crime occurs when a perpetrator targets a victim because of his or her perceived membership in a certain group. In this case, it was homosexuality.

On August 7, 1988, Stephen K. Lamie, thirty-eight, was killed at the baseball diamond at Jefferson High School. His body was found by police at 3:30 a.m. after a telephone tip. At the scene, police found that Lamie's underwear was around his legs, as if a sexual encounter had ensued. His gym shorts had been removed. He had died from trauma to his head and face. In other words, he had been beaten to death.

Lamie was a postal worker who had attended Southwestern High School and had graduated from Purdue University in 1971.

Police arrested a juvenile suspect. Because he was a juvenile, police couldn't release his name. But that changed a few days later when the teen was charged as an adult. Timothy Schick, seventeen, was accused of killing Lamie and was charged with murder, robbery resulting in serious bodily injury and confinement resulting in serious bodily injury.

The trial was held in November in Tippecanoe Superior Court, and the truth came out. Schick told his friend, John P. Hamilton, about what had happened, and Hamilton testified at the trial. Schick had woken him about 2:30 a.m. and told him that his car had broken down on Earl Avenue and that he was picked up by a man (Lamie). Schick asked Lamie if he was getting any girls and where he might find some. He later told the man he wanted oral sex, and the man said he could take care of that, according to an article in the *Lafayette Journal Courier.*

The two ended up at the ball diamond. That's where Schick beat him to death. Then he went to Hamilton's house. The Hamilton boys then returned to the ball field, where they cleaned Tim's fingerprints from the car at his request. Then they took Tim home. Hamilton's father called police with the tip but a few hours later called them back to admit that he was the one who called them. Police arrested Tim at 6:30 a.m. at his home.

At the trial, it came out that Schick had been drinking heavily the night before with a couple of friends and that he had gotten in a fight with one of them.

Apparently, when Lamie made sexual advances at Schick, he responded by beating Lamie to death to protect himself. Or at least, that's the way the jury saw it, and they found Schick guilty of voluntary manslaughter instead of murder.

Schick received a jail term of forty-four years.

TRIPLE MURDERER GETS DEATH SENTENCE

In Lafayette history, there is one triple murder that has occurred. The murderer was tried, convicted and given a lethal injection on June 13, 2003, becoming only the second person to be given the death sentence in the 1980s and executed early in the twenty-first century.

Joseph L. Trueblood had a girlfriend named Susan Bowsher. After their breakup, Susan had intentions of going back to her ex-husband, Robert Hughes of Brookston.

Joseph picked up Susan and her children on the afternoon of Monday, August 15, 1988, and drove off. Trueblood became upset with her and pulled out a .22-caliber revolver that he had taken from his father. He shot her in the head three times before turning the gun on the children and shooting them in the head as well. Ashelyn Nicole Hughes was two years old, and William Eugene Bowsher was only one year old.

Joseph then drove them to an isolated area near West Point and dumped their bodies off the side of the road.

The next morning, he went to see his twin brother, William, in Lafayette to borrow a shovel to bury the bodies. Joseph admitted to killing them to his brother. William actually saw the blood on him. Then Joseph went to bury the bodies.

Meanwhile, Susan's father reported her and the children missing. Lafayette police officers began an investigation.

William decided to call the police to tell them what his brother had done. When police officers came to question Joseph, he saw the police cars as he drove into the apartment complex and fled. Police took chase and followed him until he drove onto a dead-end street. Joseph tried to flee on foot, but officers tackled and arrested him. Police officers took note of the blood on the seats in the vehicle.

Joseph denied the murders at first and said that he hadn't seen Susan and the children in more than a week. Later, Joseph admitted to the murders and decided to show the officers where he had buried them; instead he sent them on a wild goose chase.

A day later, a farmer near West Point discovered one of the bodies and called the police. Officers came to the area and found the bodies of the three victims in the second of two pits.

A search for the murder weapon began in the Wabash River. Lafayette police officers were aided by a dozen divers from other departments. They

Joseph Trueblood buried the three bodies in the woods. A depression is still evident in the place where the bodies were buried. *Photo by author.*

looked for days until Trueblood pointed them in the right direction. He had broken down the gun into two parts and thrown them in the river. Police finally located the parts sixty feet from shore under about six feet of water.

For some unknown reason, Trueblood wanted to visit the grave sites he had dug for them, so his lawyer obtained a judge's permission. When he was interviewed for the pre-sentence report, he claimed that Susan had shot the children and then killed herself.

The trial was held in March 1990 at the Tippecanoe Circuit Court. After four witnesses had testified, Trueblood indicated a desire to plead guilty and did so. According to the *Lafayette Journal & Courier*, his court-appointed attorney, Thomas O'Brien, told the court, "We've taken the jury out of consideration and have thrown ourselves on the mercy of the court. We'll be happy with anything less than a death sentence."

At a hearing to determine if Trueblood should get the death sentence, a pathologist testified that Susan couldn't have killed herself. A bullet wound in her cheek wasn't characteristic of suicide, and she had been shot behind each ear. Also at the hearing, his family defended his honor by saying that he once saved a woman from a burning building. However, members of his family also had records of violence. One of his brothers was in prison for battery, and another was convicted of robbery. His father had abused his mother and had taught him and his four brothers how to shoot guns, but he was proud that Joseph didn't like to shoot animals.

That hearing didn't have much influence on Judge Ronald L. Melichar, who sentenced him to death on April 12. "Your conduct, Mr. Trueblood, reflects the worst in the human soul," he said. When the judge asked him if he had anything to say, he again denied his guilt.

Appeals were unsuccessful, but in August 2000 he petitioned the court for a writ of habeas corpus. Nearly one year later, U.S. district court judge Allen Sharp, Northern District of Indiana, granted habeas relief as to the murder of Susan Bowsher in that the guilty plea was involuntary because the trial court failed to advise Trueblood that by pleading guilty he would be admitting his guilt. He was also granted habeas relief because the trial court found as an aggravating circumstance that the murders were "cold blooded, premeditated killings of three helpless and defenseless persons." He ordered his release or retrial within 120 days.

A month later, his ruling was overturned and the death sentence reinstated by the U.S. Court of Appeals, Seventh Circuit.

The day before his scheduled execution, Trueblood applied for a stay, but it was denied by the parole board and by the Indiana Supreme Court. Governor Frank O'Bannon also denied him clemency. He was executed with a lethal injection at 12:24 a.m. on June 13, 2003. He was forty-six years old.

PURDUE PROFESSOR KILLS WIFE

A few murders in West Lafayette have involved Purdue University. One of the latest concerned an assistant professor at Purdue University who killed his wife.

Edgar R. Knapp Jr. was thirty-five and teaching computer science at Purdue in 1994. He lived at home in West Lafayette with his wife, Brenda L. Kasarjian, and two children. On the evening of July 24, 1994, they got into an argument that led to his wife telling him that she wanted a divorce and to get out of the house.

Edgar stated that he went to the bathroom, and when he returned to the bedroom, his wife was pointing her .38-caliber Smith & Wesson revolver at him, according to court testimony. Edgar grabbed for the gun, and they fell on the bed. "As soon as she hit the bed, the gun went off," he testified.

Brenda then pointed the gun at him again, and they struggled over it again. The gun went off again, according to him. He then said he got control of the gun and tried to point the gun away from them and fired a third shot toward the bedroom door. He didn't recall a fourth shot. "I was absolutely convinced she was trying to kill me," he said, according to a *Lafayette Journal & Courier* article.

He then called 911 and shouted to a police dispatcher, "I just shot my wife!"

Edgar's testimony didn't fit the gunshot wounds his wife received. A pathologist said earlier in the trial that bullets struck her in the left side and right breast and then went through her and directly into the bed, which means that she was shot in the back. She was also shot in the upper abdomen and the right temple. Prosecutors said that his story didn't make sense because the first two shots came from too far away for her to have any control of the gun.

The jury didn't buy into Edgar's story, either, and found him guilty of murder after less than two hours of deliberation. The judge gave him a fifty-year sentence.

In 2009, Edgar Knapp requested that the court send him back to Germany to serve the rest of his sentence there, but the request was denied, according to Tippecanoe Superior Court officials. He could be eligible for parole in 2010.

STEPMOM TORTURES DAUGHTER TO DEATH

Prisoners of war sometimes go through a lot of torture before they are killed. What a Lafayette stepmother did to her four-year-old daughter could easily be compared to what some POWs have gone through.

Aiyana was born on December 12, 2000, to Christian and Cassandra Gauvin. Christian and Cassandra parted ways, and he obtained custody of Aiyana on December 19, 2003. Then he married Michelle on February 18, 2005. Aiyana joined a family with an older brother, Eric, age nine,

Michelle Gauvin tortured her child to death. *Courtesy Lafayette Police Department.*

and an older sister, Justini, age twelve.

Aiyana's stepmother watched over her during the day, and her father watched her in the evenings. When Aiyana started exhibiting behavioral problems, her parents started punishing her. They claimed that she acted defiantly and disrespectfully to them. She urinated in bed and soiled herself. Also, they said that she refused to eat or she would eat condiments out of the refrigerator at night.

In response to Aiyana's behavior, Michelle often tied her up and put duct tape over her mouth. She bound her to a play gate or booster seat with zipper-style child cabinet safety locks. She would hit her with her hand or pieces of a wooden cutting board. When Aiyana bit her, Michelle bit her back. Aiyana was put in a small room adjacent to the house. At night, they tied the door shut and anchored a chair to it so she would not get out. The room had a bed without bedding, though she was not permitted to sleep on it. She was sometimes bound and put in the corner of the cold room. They took photos of her in bondage. In one photo, she was tied to her bed wearing an overflowing diaper and lying in her excrement, according to court papers.

On March 15, 2005, Aiyana was severely beaten while she was bound to a chair. After Michelle tried to feed her and she refused, she duct taped Aiyana's mouth and put her in the room still strapped to a booster seat. She left her like that all night.

The next morning, Michelle called 911 and reported that her four-year-old was choking. Police and emergency workers found Aiyana not breathing, lacking a pulse and cold to the touch. She had died long before they arrived. Michelle told them that she found her on the floor unconscious. The coroner arrived and said that she was "obviously deceased."

An autopsy revealed that Aiyana died from an acute subdural hematoma caused by vigorous shaking or blunt force injuries to her head within the past twenty-four hours. She had numerous bruises, abrasions and scratches covering her little body that were less than a day to several days old. The pathologist estimated that she had been struck in the head four or five times and two dozen times on the rest of her body. Aiyana had ligature marks on her wrists. She was so malnourished that she had lost body fat and had suffered liver damage. Her extremities were swollen. Even her bowels were impacted. And she was dehydrated.

The parents were taken into custody. During a search warrant of the home, police found three broken cutting boards in a kitchen drawer that had been used to beat the child.

According to court records, when corrections officer Tammy Lynch went to Michelle's cell to investigate a report of attempted suicide, she told her, "I killed the little bitch. The little bitch pissed me off and I killed her." Lynch asked Michelle if she was referring to Aiyana, and she responded, "Yes, I killed the little bitch and she deserved it, too."

On September 15, 2005, she pleaded guilty to murder and neglect of a dependent. The trial court sentenced Michelle to life in prison without parole and two twenty-four-year terms for confinement and neglect, all served consecutively. The court found two aggravating circumstances: Aiyana was less than twelve, and she was tortured while she was alive. The thirty-four-year-old mother had no prior convictions and suffered a borderline personality disorder as a result of a tragic childhood, but she had raised two other exemplary children.

Michelle was born to a married woman whose husband was not her father. Her father was an African American who was a friend. The mother had claimed that she was raped and that she was subject to heated arguments and the object of racial prejudice. At eighteen months, Michelle was put up for adoption. She was adopted by a loving couple with two equally kind sons. She attended Mayflower Mill Elementary and McCutcheon High School, where she was teased for being a biracial daughter of a white couple. She was disciplined in school for talking back. She was the subject of five protective orders and had conflicts with neighbors and boyfriends. But the court didn't feel that all of this justified what she did to her stepdaughter.

Christian, Aiyana's father, got off more fortunately. He was charged with neglect of a dependent and sentenced to fifty years in jail. Since Michelle admitted to the murder, prosecutors never went after him for murder.

However, a judge wrote the following in an appeal of the case: "I respect the determination of the trial court and my colleagues that Michelle should spend the rest of her life in prison without possibility of parole. But in my view, Christian participated in the same series of acts as Michelle and her sentence is disproportionately severe."

Michelle's appeal was denied.

PART II

WHITE COUNTY

BRADY GANG GUNS DOWN STATE TROOPER

The nation was still in the grip of the Great Depression in 1937. Many banks had gone belly up. Jobs were scarce. Money was in short supply.

The Brady gang was driving around Illinois and Indiana robbing stores, filling stations, drugstores and banks. The FBI had placed them on the Most Wanted List. Director J. Edgar Hoover described them as one of the most vicious and dangerous gangs in history.

In May, the gang was hanging out in Baltimore when they began to run short of money, so they decided to go to the Midwest for funds. They drove to Sheldon, Illinois, to rob a bank there but found that it was already out of business. So they turned their attention to the bank in Goodland. They hit it on May 25 and took $2,528, a good sum of money in those days.

As they were making their getaway, they spotted a state police car near Royal Center and fired upon it. The state policeman gave chase.

The gang drove their stolen Ford around behind the United Methodist Church at the crossroads of State Road 16 and County Road 1450 East along the Cass County line, so it was out of sight. Gang leader Alfred Brady grabbed a machine gun, while Clarence Lee Schaffer Jr. and George Dalhover took rifles. A few minutes later, State Police Officer Paul Vincent Minneman, with Deputy Sheriff Elmer Craig of Cass County in his car,

This historical marker was placed on Indiana 16 in 1992 to honor Paul Vincent Minneman, who was shot to death there in 1937 by the Brady gang. The Calley United Methodist Church is still in use today. *Photo by author.*

pulled up to the front of the church. The officers exited the car and tried to determine where the gang had gone.

The gang opened fire on the police officers. Minneman was riddled with bullets and fell dead, while Craig staggered from the other side of the car, badly wounded.

Schaffer walked over to the wounded officer and said to the others, "Shall I finish this guy, too?"

"No, come on, let's get the hell out of here!" replied Brady, according to a *Monticello Herald Journal* article.

Schaffer grabbed the sheriff's shotgun and handcuffs, while Dalhover removed Minneman's belt, holster and the medicine kit. They left the deputy to bleed to death. The three took the loot in their car and drove back to Baltimore.

They left behind the first Indiana state trooper to die from a criminal's bullet. In fact, he had been pierced by twenty bullets. Also left behind was Minneman's wife with their unborn child, Pauline. Craig also died.

The FBI caught up to the Brady gang later that year in Bangor, Maine. Brady and Schaffer were killed by the feds during a robbery attempt, while Dalhover was taken into custody. He was brought back to Indiana and convicted of killing Minneman. Dalhover was electrocuted on November 18, 1938, at Indiana State Penitentiary in Michigan City.

In 1992, the Indiana Historical Bureau erected a historical marker at the site of the gun battle.

CUB SCOUT GETS SHOT TO DEATH

Sammy Joe Moss was born on August 19, 1949, in nearby Lafayette. His mother and father were Alma and Sam C. Moss. The family later moved to Monticello, where Sammy grew up.

Sammy was just five when his mother and father split up. His father left for California after the divorce. His mother began seeing other men. In 1957, his mother met a man by the name of Albert M. Colvin Jr. She worked at Bryan Manufacturing at the time, and Al sometimes had a job laying ceramic tile or working at a nearby service station. He had formerly lived in Kokomo. Before that, he had served in the army for ten years, with a tour of duty in Europe during World War II, where he was with an artillery outfit.

They lived together at her home at 617 West Harrison along with Sammy's older sister, Anna Marie, and older brother, Bob. Sammy Joe attended fourth grade at the South Elementary School. He had many friends at school and was well liked by all.

In November 1957, Sammy joined the Cub Scouts. A year later, he was given his Denner stripes.

Many times, Anna Marie would have to watch over Sammy. And sometimes he would wander away from the house and go downtown, which was less than a mile away. "He'd go downtown and buy candy and put it on mom's account," she explained in an interview.

One time he went downtown, and she found him peddling this little tractor down Main Street. He had taken it from a store on Main Street. "I had a fit," she said.

Al played with Sammy more than he did with the older children in the family. He'd play catch with the boy or take him to the playground at times. Al didn't get along with the older son, Robert, a senior at Twin Lakes High

This photo of the Moss family was taken on April 6, 1956. Standing over Samuel Joe were his brother Robert E., mother Alma S. and sister Anna Marie. *Courtesy of Anna Marie Moss Anderson.*

School. And Anna Marie, age sixteen, started staying away from him more and more. "If he ate in the kitchen, I would eat in the living room," she explained. Her boyfriend, Joe Hughes, also had a disagreement with Al. Neither of them wanted to be around Al.

On New Year's Eve 1958, Anna Marie and her boyfriend wanted to go play cards with another couple, but an ice storm was raining down on the city. Al wanted some liquor, so they agreed to take him to the liquor store to get some. On the way out the door, Al slipped and fell on the slippery porch. "That tickled me," said Anna Marie.

Anna Marie and her boyfriend decided not to go out that night and stayed at home to play games with Al and her mother. When they decided to play a board game, Al got mad at Anna Marie as she tried to explain the rules. They argued. The game ended. "My mom gave me a nerve pill," said Anna Marie.

The next day, Anna Marie asked her mother if she could get married. Her mother would not consent as Anna Marie was just a junior at Twin Lakes High School.

Her mother kicked Al out of the house for a few days and told him that he needed to stop drinking. Al stopped by the McCall Texaco Station to get his paycheck. He had worked on and off at the station since it had opened in May 1958. While there, he stole a .22-caliber automatic Astra pistol.

On Saturday, January 9, 1959, Anna Marie had gone to the dentist and had her rotten teeth pulled so she could get false teeth. When Monday came along, Anna Marie didn't feel much like going to school, so she stayed at home. Al spent the day at a local tavern.

When her mother got home from work, Alma went about making a fresh pot of coffee to sober up Albert, who had been drinking all day. Her boyfriend came into the kitchen and asked Alma, "What are you doing that for?"

"I want some coffee," she explained, according to a *Monticello Herald Journal* article. "You need some coffee."

Anna Marie decided that she didn't want to be in the same house with her mother's drunken boyfriend, so they left to go to his boyfriend's mother's house. They headed to his car. "I saw my little brother [Sammy Joe] coming and I thought about taking him with, but he had Scouts." They left without him at about 4:00 p.m.

About 4:30 p.m., some Cub Scouts from Den 5 of Cub Scout Pack 328 started arriving for a 5:00 p.m. meeting at the Moss house. Alma was the den mother. Sammy Joe greeted the Cub Scouts as they arrived. They included Bobby Burns, Billy Morris and Tim Bernfield. The boys sat in the living room and watched television while waiting for the other Scouts to arrive.

Meanwhile, Al and Alma got into an argument in the kitchen. Alma spotted a gun in Al's pocket and feared for her life. She ran out to the living room to call police. She picked up the phone and yelled, "94, 94" to the operator. That was the number for the police department.

Al grabbed the phone and replaced the receiver. She picked up the receiver and Al grabbed it again. She did it a third time, and Al pulled out the gun he had stolen from the service station. He turned to the Scouts and yelled, "Get out!"

The three Scouts left the house like it was on fire. As they came out of the house, they ran into more Scouts arriving at the house, including Kean MacOwan. "We ran to the police station for help," he said in an interview.

Meanwhile, Sammy Joe ran toward his mother. Al was aiming for her belly and fired; the bullet struck the boy in the back of the head. Al fired again and hit Alma in the head. Then Al turned the gun on himself and fired at his own head. He grazed his forehead and fell to the floor. His wound only stunned him.

Bob "Billy" Musall was the first officer to arrive at the Sammy Joe Moss murder scene. *Courtesy of Bob Musall.*

The Cub Scouts told Shirley, who was delivering the newspaper, what was happening. She rode to the police station on her bike as fast as her little legs would carry her.

Meanwhile, a neighbor called police. "We received a call from someone that they heard shots," recalled Bob Musall, who was on duty at the police station. "Back then we had a telephone operator. I tired to call back, but didn't get a hold of anyone."

Then the newspaper carrier arrived at the station and told Officer Musall what had happened.

"I rushed to the scene and ran into the home," explained Bob in an interview. "I saw a gun in his [Albert] hand and kicked it out of the way. He was faking death."

Then he turned his attention to Sammy Joe and his mother. "I ran over to the boy," he remembered. "I knew he was dead." Red blood was splattered on his blue uniform. He thought Alma was dead, as well. She lay next to the telephone stand. Musall then picked up Albert, handcuffed him and took him away. He also called for an ambulance and backup.

Bob, Sammy's older brother, had been working at Kroger. A minister picked him up there and gave him the news. The minister took him home. When Bob entered the home, he saw that Sammy Joe's body was still lying on the floor. His mother had already been taken to the White County Memorial Hospital in Monticello. Bob was shocked at the scene. Then the ambulance from the Miller Funeral Home took Sammy Joe away.

About an hour after the murder, Sammy's sister, Anna Marie, received some of the news while at her boyfriend's home. The police had called Joe's father and explained what had happened. Anna Marie overheard him say, "And he shot himself, too?" She knew something had happened. Her boyfriend told her to go out to the car.

When Joe got to town, he pulled up to the Monticello Police Department. "Why don't you come in," he told her. He took her into the police station and introduced her, "This is Alma Moss's daughter."

"I asked the officer about Sammy Joe, and the guy behind the counter could hardly face me," Anna Marie explained. "I didn't know my brother was involved until then." She went with her boyfriend to stay at his sister's home.

When police interviewed Al, he admitted that he stole the pistol from the service station and had intended to kill his girlfriend, but he claimed that the shooting of the boy was accidental. He also signed a confession to the crimes and the wounding of himself. The preliminary charge by prosecutor Fred Schwanke was first-degree murder. He was arraigned in city court on that charge and held without bail.

Sam Moss, the father of Sammy Joe, arrived in Monticello on Wednesday evening from California. Sam decided not to take his children back to California so that they could finish out the school year. Instead, they would stay at their great-grandmother's home, also in Monticello.

On Thursday, the White County Grand Jury convened. It had been seven years since the last grand jury had been held. The jury consisted of three men and three women: Willard Geisler, Liberty Township; Roy Keller, West Point Township; William Haff, Prairie Township; Jean Klinkhamer, Union Township; Edith Baer, Lincoln Township; and Mary Westerhouse, Union Township. Keller was the jury foreman, and Walter Simons was the special grand jury bailiff.

The next day, funeral services were held for Sammy Joe at the Pike Creek Church. Reverend Leroy Vick performed the service. Several who attended the funeral still live in Monticello, including Neil Smith, owner of N. Smith Jewelry, who was in his Cub Scout troop. He will never forget seeing Sammy Joe in his Scout uniform in the coffin. "We had a lot of fun together," recalled Smith in an interview. He was age ten at the time. Sammy Joe was buried at Riverview Cemetery, which overlooks Monticello from across Lake Freeman. The cemetery is run by the International Order of Odd Fellows.

Sammy Joe Moss was dressed in his scouting uniform in the casket. *Courtesy of Anna Marie Moss Anderson.*

On Saturday, Al was transferred from the Monticello jail to a more suitable facility, the Cass County jail in Logansport. The Monticello jail had four cells back then located in what is now the fire station. White County had no jail at the time.

The grand jury interviewed nine witnesses and took three days to determine what to do with Al. On Monday, members of the jury returned two indictments: first-degree murder and assault and battery with intent to commit murder in the first degree. Sheriff Charles G. Miller read the charges to Al in Logansport. Judge Russell Gordon assigned attorney Robert Million as a public defender to represent Al, who had no money to hire an attorney.

On Wednesday, Al and his attorney appeared before Judge Gordon. Al pleaded guilty to the first-degree murder of Sammy Joe. Then his attorney requested some leniency for his client because he had pleaded guilty. The other charge was dropped, even though Alma was lying in a coma at the hospital. Judge Gordon didn't take long to pronounce sentence: life imprisonment. It was the first time he had imposed such a sentence in his twenty-one years on the bench. Al sat silent in the courtroom with his head bowed in shame. The judge could have given him the death sentence. "You still have an opportunity to do many things you haven't done and get right with God," the judge said, according to the *Monticello Herald Journal*.

The next day, Al was transferred from the Cass County jail to the state prison in Michigan City. He would have to serve a minimum of fifteen years before becoming eligible for parole.

News of the tragic death of the Cub Scout spread all over the world as United Press International and the Associated Press picked up on the story. It was even printed in the *Pacific Stars and Stripes*, a military newspaper in Japan. Letters of condolence came pouring in, and a wreath was sent all the way from Toronto, Canada.

Alma was in a coma for about a week at White County Memorial Hospital in north Monticello. Then she was semi-comatose. In February, Alma was taken to a hospital in Indianapolis. In May, she underwent surgery. "All they could do was remove bone fragments," explained Anna Marie.

After the surgery, Alma was sent to the Longcliff Mental Hospital in Logansport for therapy. She was able to walk a little bit but was very unstable, so she used a walker. She also began saying words—just "hi" and "bye" at first. Her progress was as slow as a child learning how to walk and talk for the first time. She finally progressed to just using a cane to help her walk.

When the school year ended, Sammy Joe's brother and sister went to Whittier (now LaMirada), California, to live with their father. "I talked him into getting married," explained Anna Marie. So she returned to Monticello to marry Joe Hughes and finish out her senior year at Twin Lakes High School.

Sometime later, Louise Watkins Hacker wrote a poem about the tragedy and gave it to Anna Marie. It was titled "Little Scout—Sammy Joe":

Dear little Scout, so brave and true
Busy and happy just being "you."
Eyes a sparkle with small boy plans;
Little you knew of the shifting sands.

Head held high in the scout salute,
Proud to be part of your Boy Scout troop
Busy hands tying those difficult knots
Learning to make those Boy Scout cots.

A real good boy, our Sammy Joe,
Asking questions and wanting to know
How to gain courage and live just right.
Kneeling in prayer to God each night.

Learning the rules of the Boy Scout book,
All of these things our Sammy took
Within his heart so filled with love.
He gave of himself as his Lord above.

Walking in paths the Master trod
Little life filled with the love of God.
As died his Jesus upon the tree
So died Sammy to save "Mommy."

Dear little scout, from out the blue
Our Lord came down to comfort you
Cradled in the arms of his great love
Our Sammy has gone to live above.

The cares of the world are his no more,
His feet have traveled another shore.
To brighten the way to Heaven's gate
Our Sammy's reward, eternally great.

Then one Christmas in the early 1970s, Alma went missing. "I went there and she wasn't there," explained Anna Marie. Her aunt in Logansport had been keeping tabs on her mother. Her aunt knew that she would show up back at the state hospital to pick up her Social Security check the first of the month.

Her aunt called her in January and told her, "I just saw your mother, and she just got married."

Alma had married Billy Stevens, who was also living at the state hospital in Logansport. "We didn't recognize the marriage," said Anna Marie. "It was a very uncomfortable situation."

In 1974, a parole officer came to Monticello to test the waters for releasing Al, who had served fifteen years in prison and was eligible for parole. He first went to the police station and was told that he wouldn't be safe in town, according to Anna Marie. Then he came to see her. "I'm going to tell you my true feelings," said Anna Marie. "My mother will suffer the rest of her life—an invalid. As far as I'm concerned, he needs to pay as much as she suffers—the rest of her life." Alvin was not paroled, as far as Anna Marie knows.

Alma Sarah Hare Moss is buried next to her son, Samuel Joe Moss, at Riverview Cemetery in east Monticello. *Photo by author.*

Another time, a parole officer came to the Monticello Police as amnesty was being considered for Albert. The police spread out all the bloody crime scene photos for the parole officer to see, Anna Marie explained. Amnesty was not granted by the governor.

In the 1980s, Alma's health was diminishing, and she had to revert to a wheelchair. She was admitted to a nursing home. Both she and her husband Billy lived there together, but Alma wanted to leave her husband and told Anna Marie to help. When she tried to help her mother, her mother changed her mind. "He probably took advantage of her," Anna Marie said.

In the early 1990s, Anna Marie got a call from her sister-in-law. She had found a devotional book, and one of the devotions had to do with Sammy Joe. This woman was passing through Monticello at the time of the murder.

Now many of the people involved in this story have passed away. Anna Marie's first husband, Joe Hughes, died in 1993. Alma died on February 20, 2002. She was seventy-seven. Robert Moss, sixty-six, died on June 25, 2007, in Santa Clara, California. He was buried there at Mission City Memorial Park.

At the time of her mother's death, Anna Marie was living in Tennessee, but she moved back to White County in 2002. After her first husband passed, Anna Marie married her present husband, Don, who she was friends with in high school. Her husband runs Liberty Signs out of his farmstead. She is now sixty-seven years old, and they live in northeast White County near Buffalo.

Before Christmas 2008, Anna Marie contacted Monticello Cub Scout Pack 3154 so she could make a donation to help purchase uniforms or other items for needy Scouts. She plans on doing this annually.

Today, Anna Marie thinks differently about what happened. "It took me a long time to come to terms with it," she explained. "God does things for a reason."

She doesn't know what happened to Albert Colvin. "If I had spoken to him, I would have asked him why?" Colvin died on April 27, 2004, and is buried in Churubusco, Indiana, which is northwest of Fort Wayne.

BURGLARY TURNS INTO MURDER

In April 1974, Monticello was devastated by a category-four tornado. The downtown area was literally ripped apart. Easy access to buildings led to looting and robbing. One burglary even led to a murder.

On the morning of Monday, June 17, three burglaries occurred in downtown Monticello. One happened at Sixbey's Tru-Value Store Hardware at 501 North Main Street. Another occurred at Miller's Department Store at 103 North Main Street. A third happened at Hively's Pharmacy at 101 West Broadway.

The one at Hively's was the most devastating. While two burglars were ransacking the pharmacy for drugs and goods, Victor Tull came to work shortly after 6:00 a.m. He lived a few blocks away on Bluff Street. He was a janitor at the store and was hired by Ron Hively, the owner.

Tull discovered two burglars inside the store. One of the burglars shot him not once, not twice, but three times. Tull turned to the burglar and said, "Don't shoot me no more!" The burglar didn't, and they ran from the store. Tull soon died.

"He pleaded for his life, and they shot him again and killed him," recalled Bob Fox, who was a detective sergeant for the Indiana State Police at the time and investigated the case.

Hively's Pharmacy was located at the corner of Main Street and Broadway in downtown Monticello. *Courtesy of the White County Historical Society.*

Tull's body was discovered a little after 7:00 a.m. when Mike Culross, a pharmacist, came to work at Hively's. He thought that Tull might have suffered a heart attack and called the Monticello Police and Fire Departments at 7:15 a.m. When police arrived, they discovered that Tull had been shot in the back three times.

"I'll never forget seeing him lying on the floor," Fox remembered.

Fox, along with the Monticello Police Department and the White County sheriff's department, began their investigation by setting up a road block at the corner of Main Street and Broadway and questioning everyone. Someone told them about an orange late-model car that had been parked near the Monticello United Methodist Church and that had sped off early that morning. Witnesses told police that they saw two black males running through the alley. No blacks lived in Monticello at the time, according to the census, so that would rule out any locals.

The police discovered that the burglars had come in through an empty second-floor apartment. They also found a trail of items left along the alley

Above: Leonard Daneau had a Fu Manchu–like mustache when he was taken into custody. *Courtesy White County Sheriff's Department.*

Below: Jack Laird had a full beard and long locks when he was taken into custody. *Courtesy White County Sheriff's Department.*

while the burglars were fleeing. Some camera and stereo equipment were found, as well as a bottle of Quaalude tranquilizers. Quaaludes were a common item being stolen from drugstores at the time.

On Wednesday, the sixty-six-year-old Tull was laid to rest. He was buried at Tippecanoe Memory Gardens. Tull was born and raised in Lafayette. He attended Battle Ground High School and worked for twenty-five years at Ross Gear Division of TRW Automotive in Lafayette before retiring in 1959. He had moved to Monticello in 1968. He was married to Gertrude Reynolds.

Police developed a list of suspects, and one was a man by the name of Jack Lee Laird, whose legal last name was Brant. "We checked on Laird, and the vehicle ended up matching," explained Fox in an interview; he was with the state police from 1956 until 1980. Laird had an orange 1973 Monte Carlo.

On Thursday, about twenty police officers moved in on their suspects in Lafayette and Crawfordsville. They arrested Laird and Leonard R. Daneau and charged them with first-degree murder.

They also arrested Daneau's wife, Barbara S., and charged her with several crimes: accessory after the fact to murder and burglary and receiving stolen goods. Three others were charged with being accessories: Jacki S. Louden, Alan Van Pelt and Morris W. Kairts. Daneau and Laird were held in the White County jail without bond. Leading the investigation were Fox and Monticello patrolman Norm Thompson.

Police found many of the goods that the thieves had taken. What the police didn't have was the gun used in the killing, a .25-caliber automatic pistol.

On Saturday, police arrested a Monon man by the name of Branson Clark and charged him with accessory after the fact to first-degree murder.

On June 25, Van Pelt pleaded guilty to visiting a common nuisance (a place where illegal drugs are sold), although he was originally charged with accessory after the fact. He was fined $500 and given a six-month sentence suspended. Laird and Daneau went to Van Pelt's home after the pharmacy robbery.

Ten days after the murder, police found the murder weapon at a farm in Jasper County. It had been torched in an effort to erase the serial number. Police also found a .45-caliber semiautomatic rifle.

Prosecutor L.D. Dellinger Jr. waited until July 5 to assemble a grand jury, because that's when the jury was drawn for the next three months.

On July 10, two of the arrested pleaded guilty. Clark and Louden both admitted to being accessories after the fact to second-degree burglary. Two weeks later, Judge Maurice Zerface sentenced both of them to two- to five-year sentences but suspended Louden's entire sentence and placed her on probation. She had fully cooperated with police and led them to several other burglaries in Tippecanoe County. Zerface suspended nine months of the minimum two-year sentence for Clark. Of the remaining fifteen months, Clark got credited for a month in jail and got two months taken off from his sentence for good behavior, so Clark would have to serve at least another year in jail. Clark also had cooperated with police and agreed to testify in the murder charges against Laird and Daneau. Laird had borrowed two guns from Clark. One was the murder weapon.

Charges against Kairts were dropped and he was released.

On July 30, Laird pleaded innocent to the second-degree murder charge and requested a jury trial through his attorney, E. Kent Moore of Lafayette.

On the other hand, Leonard Daneau pleaded guilty to commission of a felony while armed with a deadly or dangerous weapon. His wife, Barbara, also pleaded guilty to one of the six counts against her.

A week later, Deputy Prosecutor Robert Thacker recommended the minimum ten-year sentence for Leonard Daneau, and Judge Zerface agreed. When the judge asked him if he had anything to say for himself, he responded, "No, sir, just I'm sorry for what happened."

Barbara Daneau, age twenty-eight, received a two- to five-year sentence in the women's prison. The other five charges were still pending against her, however. They were later dropped.

Now attention turned to Laird. He was born in Lafayette on April 2, 1953, to Dorothy Brissey. His father, whose last name was Brant, died when he was young. His mother remarried a Laird. Both of his parents drank and fought often. Jack turned to crime as a juvenile and had a long record. He dropped out of school in the tenth grade and ended up in the Indiana Boys School. Then he turned eighteen and married Debra Soloman. They had two children, Shanon and Jack Jr., before their marriage ended in divorce in April 1974.

The jury trial for Laird was scheduled for October 28; however, he decided to plead guilty to the charge on September 10. A few days later, Judge Zerface sentenced him to fifteen to twenty-five years in prison. The judge ordered him to go to a diagnostic center in Plainfield first before prison. The judge said in court, "He could be getting life and, if not for the plea bargaining that was made, I would see that he would get life."

Laird's attorney, Moore, was impressed with the criminal investigation and said that Fox should be "highly commended." Fox didn't attribute the investigation all to himself. "That was where all the departments came together," Fox commented. "Not any one person solved that one."

Laird admitted to the court that he had taken a large amount of drugs before the burglary spree that morning. He had been staying with the Daneaus for a couple of days, taking Demerol and reds (barbiturates) by injection. When he saw Tull chasing after his accomplice, he fired at Tull to stop him. He fired four shots in all, three striking Tull in the back. He also admitted to committing more then two hundred burglaries in northern Indiana, but he wasn't being tried for those lesser crimes.

The hippie-looking Laird, who had hair so long he wore it in two ponytails on the back of his head, gave a photographer from the *Monticello Herald Journal* a peace sign as he sat in a police car on his way to the Michigan City Prison.

Two years later on April 14, Leonard Daneau took his life in prison at age thirty-two. He attached his belt to a bar and committed suicide.

In 1977, Laird pleaded for clemency from his prison cell. The request was denied by the governor. The following year, he petitioned White County Court for a release because he felt that his attorney was incompetent. He also had some new evidence that had been supplied by prison inmates who had spoken to Daneau before he killed himself. Judge Karl Overbook declared that Laird's attorney had been competent and that information from other prisoners would be hearsay, since Daneau was dead.

In 1979, Laird filed an appeal. It was denied. Then his attorney filed for a modification of his sentence. It, too, was denied. On January 24, 1980, he applied for a work release. It was denied.

At some point in 1983, Laird got out of prison on good behavior, but he went back to being a criminal. On December 12, 1983, he was found guilty of possession and dealing of a controlled substance in Tippecanoe County. He wasn't in jail for long though, because Fox asked him to come speak to a group called Youth and Law Enforcement (YALE) when he was chief of police in Monticello. "He told them he had found God and reformed himself."

Two days later, Laird was busted for robbing another drugstore in Valparaiso, Fox recalled. So much for reform. He was given a four-year sentence.

Two years later, Laird was busted again for theft and receiving stolen property in Tippecanoe County. He was given eight years for those two crimes and wouldn't be eligible for parole until 1994.

Where he is today is anybody's guess.

Fox went on to serve as the mayor of the city. Now retired, he still lives in Monticello. "That was such an unnecessary killing," Fox concluded.

LOVE TRIANGLE RESULTS IN MURDER

The murder case talked about the most in Monticello is the one in which a wife shot her husband to death back in 1975.

Born on April 16, 1932, in Salisbury, Missouri, Wilma Lois Welch went on to Northeastern Missouri University in Kirksville after high school. After three years at the university, Lois, as she liked to be called, was well on her way to being a teacher when she met Richard Cobb. Dick was in college himself and studying to be an orthopedic surgeon. He was born in Springfield, Illinois, on February 7, 1929.

They married on August 10, 1952, and moved to Carson City, Michigan, so he could complete his degree. She was content to be Mrs. Richard Cobb and terminated her college education. She soon became pregnant and gave birth to

Michael. While Dick was finishing up his degree, he had an affair with a fellow student, but Lois knew nothing of it. She was busy raising their baby boy.

After he finished his degree, Dick decided to take up medicine in the small city of Monticello, Indiana, in 1955. He had fallen in love with the city of five thousand on a trip through it once before. Monticello was a typical small Indiana community. The city had some industry and was surrounded by farming. The RCA plant employed more than a thousand workers and kept the city prosperous. Nearby was an amusement park called Indiana Beach, and thousands flocked there during the summer. It also employed many workers. Many other people came to the area in the summer to enjoy the twin lakes, Shafer and Freeman. And some lived around the lakes all year long in expensive homes.

The Cobbs purchased a house in the Oak Park addition. Dick took off on his own practice and became an osteopath. He opened his own office on 105 West Washington Street and started practicing.

In 1959, Lois gave birth to their second child, and they named her Julie. Lois kept busy raising two children, while Dick kept busy taking care of patients. He would work hard and wouldn't come home until the last patient was seen.

Dr. Cobb liked his female clients a little too much. Once when he was treating a male patient, the two were talking one day in his lobby, and a curvy blonde came walking down the street past his office. The doctor commented, "That one has got a great little figure; I make the ones like that undress even when there is no real reason for it." Then Dr. Cobb nudged his male patient and laughed. The patient, who didn't want to be named, laughed along with him.

Dr. Cobb joined the Monticello Chamber of Commerce and served on the committee to elect a new president in 1963. He was also a member of the American Osteopathic Association and the Tippecanoe Country Club, where he would golf when he had time for the game. He was also affiliated with the White County Memorial Hospital.

On Halloween 1963, the Cobbs went to see *Holiday on Ice* at the Indiana State Fairgrounds in Indianapolis. Hoosiers from all over the state had come to see the show. The show was going along just fine and about to end when an explosion ripped through the coliseum. Bodies were flying all over. Dr. Cobb and Marvin Stewart, a funeral director from Monon, went to work immediately on those who had survived the explosion and needed help. In all, seventy-four people died in the tragedy, and more than four hundred were injured.

Dr. Richard D. Cobb's former office on Washington Street is now occupied by the White County Association of Realtors, Inc. *Photo by author.*

In 1971, Dr. Cobb had some political ambitions and ran for the county council as a Republican. He lost the election but received some publicity from the campaign.

Somewhere along the way, he became a bit too involved with a couple of his patients and had two more affairs. Meanwhile, Lois was busy caring for their two children, playing bridge, golfing, swimming and sunning herself. She also volunteered at the Monticello Library to help with disabled children. Little did she know that Dick was involved with other women until she somehow found out.

On April 3, 1974, a tornado ripped through Monticello. The downtown area was devastated, but Dick's office and home were untouched. However, power was out throughout the city, and the community was in disarray. Julie's high school had been hit, and school was suspended for a few days until other arrangements could be made. The town recovered enough in a couple of weeks to allow Dick to see patients again at his office.

On July 17, Dick decided to leave home and stay with his girlfriend, Janet Chamberlain. His departure was a total shock to Lois.

After Dick left, Lois soon became very depressed. She finally saw a couple of psychiatrists for her depression. She also took up drinking and taking pills again and was not eating right. She withdrew and would sit in the dark and keep to herself. Julie didn't know what to do. "If I had known better, I would have had intervention do something," Julie said, reflecting on the past in an interview.

Julie feels that after her parents split it was too much for her mother to take. She thinks that her mother felt humiliated, embarrassed and rejected. She said that friends rejected her mother, too. "She was Mrs. Richard Cobb," Julie explained.

On August 30, she snapped. She got a .22-caliber rifle from the closet and threatened to take her life. Julie called Reverend Edwin Helm from the Methodist church. He made arrangements to have her committed to Methodist Hospital in Indianapolis for her depression. She was there for one week.

Then, on October 26, Dick left for good on Julie's birthday. "I didn't see it coming," she said. At the time, Julie was a junior at Twin Lakes High School, a cheerleader and a member of the girls' varsity track team. The sixteen-year-old student was so "self-absorbed" in her own life that she didn't see the problem between her parents. Her brother, Mike, was a senior at Purdue University and didn't live at home. He, too, was absorbed in his life and didn't know what was going on back at home.

On November 4, the divorce papers were filed with the court and listed an "irretrievable breakdown" as the reason for the divorce, according to court records. Dick had hired Robert W. Thacker to act as his attorney in the case.

Lois was committed on November 6 to Methodist Hospital for an "emotional disorder," according to court records. Helen Kay Fisher and Reverend Edwin Helm told Judge White of the White County Circuit Court that she was of unsound mind, and White signed the order. Lewis D. Dellinger, the prosecuting attorney, signed the affidavit. What Julie didn't know at the time was that her mother had actually obtained a .38-caliber revolver from an aide at the hospital.

Lois was to appear in court on November 12, but she couldn't do that as she was still in the hospital. She hired two attorneys to represent her: Edgar W. Bayliff of Bayliff, Harrigan, Cord and Maugans and John Guy of Siferd, Roth, Christopher and Guy. Dr. James A. Hunt asked for an extension on November 20.

On December 13, Lois spoke to Dr. Hunt at St. Vincent's Hospital in Lafayette. After the talk, he discharged her from the hospital.

On December 19, Lois and Dick appeared in court for the divorce case. Lois was given custody of Julie, the home and the 1970 Oldsmobile. She also would receive $150 per week in child support. The trial was set for March 25.

When Lois returned, she still wasn't in her right mind. Although she had split from her husband, he wrote some prescriptions for her, but when she went to the pharmacy to get them filled, the druggist refused because he felt that the pills might kill her, according to Julie.

Lois began telling some close friends of hers that she was going to kill her husband. Not everyone took her seriously. One former friend of hers said that she was "insanely jealous." Another friend actually called Dick and told him that he should leave town and leave now! Dick didn't want to leave town. He had a girlfriend and a thriving practice to take care of, so he wasn't going anywhere.

On Friday, January 17, after Julie went off to school, Lois put the Smith & Wesson revolver in her coat pocket and went to her husband's office. It was crowded with patients, however, so she left instead of waiting around to see him.

After the weekend was over, Lois returned to her husband's office on Monday. Again, it was crowded with patients, so she didn't stay.

On Tuesday, January 21, Lois prepared breakfast for Julie before sending her off to school. She put on the coat containing the revolver. Instead of going to her husband's office right away, Lois went to a friend's home to talk to her about her daughter. Afterward, she drove her Oldsmobile to her husband's office in downtown Monticello.

Upon arriving at the office, she was greeted by his receptionist, Eva Marion. Another patient was there waiting for her husband, so Eva showed her to an inner waiting room instead of the front lobby. When the last patient left around noon, Eva showed Lois back to her husband's office. Then the receptionist left to go to lunch.

The couple talked for a few minutes. Lois was serious, but Dick wasn't and laughed at her. That made her even angrier. She pulled out the revolver she had in her coat pocket. Dick, who was sitting behind his big desk, could hardly believe she was serious. She pulled the trigger and shot him in the left shoulder.

Dick tried crawling under his desk to get away from her. Lois simply walked around the desk and shot him again. The bullet passed between his shoulder blades and exited through his throat. He died almost instantly.

Lois put the gun back into her coat and proceeded to her car. Nobody heard the shots, but Ralph Strik at the shoe repair shop on Illinois Street saw her leave the office and drive away in her light green 1971 Oldsmobile 98.

She drove a half-mile down the street to 306 North Fourth Street, the house of Dick's girlfriend. She entered Janet Chamberlain's home through the unlocked patio door. She found Janet in the living room with the stereo blaring.

"Turn the damn thing down!" Lois demanded, according to court records.

Janet was shocked to see Lois and did what she was asked.

"Do you know who I am?" Lois asked

"Yes, you're Dr. Cobb's wife," she nervously replied.

"You don't have to be told that I'll always be Mrs. Richard Cobb, which you will never be," Lois angrily said.

Janet remained silent and scared.

"I've never heard anything good about you," Lois said. "You're just a whore!"

"Listen, I didn't want to hurt anybody," Janet replied. "I'm sorry, but I'm in love with your husband."

"You've ruined my life, his life, my kid's lives."

"I didn't—"

"Dick is dead!"

With that, Lois pulled the gun from her pocket. As soon as Janet saw the gun, she ran out the door and through the carport toward her neighbor's house.

Lois was not far behind and fired at her. The bullet passed through Janet's hand, but she kept running. She hardly felt it. When she arrived at her neighbor's home, she realized that she had been shot. She barged into her neighbor's home and locked the door behind her.

Lois gave up the pursuit and ran to her car instead. She drove off and headed toward Carroll County. She just wanted to get away from Monticello.

Janet's neighbor called the Monticello Police Department to report the shooting and get medical help. When Police Chief Willie Green arrived with a couple of other officers, Janet told him that Lois had killed Dick. So the officers went to his office, where they found Dick lying in a pool of blood.

The police feared further violence and decided to protect Julie and Mike. Mike was on a school field trip at Purdue when he was greeted by police. "We need Michael Cobb," said an officer.

Mike's response was, "She's killed my father." He was right.

Mike got a fraternity brother to give him a ride back to Monticello. When he arrived in Monticello, police were waiting for him and escorted him to

Dr. Richard D. Cobb has a plain marker at the Riverview Cemetery. *Photo by author.*

where his sister was located, a safe house. She had been in high school at the time of the shooting.

Meanwhile, Lois drove for a while and stopped in the country near the town of Battle Ground. There she got out of her car and debated what to do next. Hours later, she finally decided to shoot herself in the left shoulder. Then she threw the gun in the woods and headed to the nearby house of Richard Roth for medical help. Roth called the state police, who arrived with an ambulance at 5:05 p.m. to take her to Lafayette for medical help.

Chief Green also arrived at Roth's house and looked at Lois's car. He found blood on the front seat and a hole through it leading to the back seat. There he spotted the lead slug lying free in the back seat. He left it there and called for a wrecker to tow the car back to Monticello to have it impounded until a search warrant could be issued.

In the meantime, State Police Officer Bob Fox went to look for the gun. He found a farmer who told him where he might find the gun, because he had seen her car pulled off the road nearby. Fox found the gun in a pile of leaves and snow. It was missing four bullets. He was certain that it was the gun that had killed Dr. Cobb and wounded his girlfriend.

The following day, Dr. Cobb's body was taken to Marion County General Hospital for an autopsy, performed by Dr. Higino Esparza. He determined quite readily that the bullet between the shoulder blades that had exited through the thorax was the one that killed him. Perhaps anyone could have figured that one out. He also found that the bullet that hit Cobb in the left shoulder broke his collarbone.

On Thursday from 4:00 to 9:00 p.m., friends of Dr. Cobb went to see him at the United Methodist Church.

The next day, services for him were held at the church, with Reverend Edwin Helm officiating. Then he was taken to Riverview Cemetery for burial.

Mike couldn't care for his sister, so Julie was taken care of by an aunt and uncle (Dr. Glen Cobb) in Providence, Kentucky.

On the Monday after the murder, White County Circuit Court convened a grand jury of six men and two women: Richard D. Martin, Jack J. Ostheimer, James R. Sharp, Charles G. Hood, Donald E. Parks, Herbert Alvin Olson, Jeanne Stangle and Shirley B. Gaudreau. Over the next three days, they heard testimony from twenty-three witnesses either in person or on videotape.

On Thursday, the jury first conferred with Judge Maurice Zerface before they turned in their two-count indictment: first-degree murder and assault and battery with intent to kill. The grand jury was dismissed at 10:30 a.m.

Thacker took the warrant to Lois's attorney, John "Jack" Guy. He drove to Lafayette to deliver the news to his client, who was still under twenty-four-hour guard at St. Elizabeth Hospital. She was recovering from her gunshot wound and was listed in satisfactory condition.

Judge Zerface had yet to determine where to put the woman. He felt that she needed a maximum-security location with medical and psychiatric facilities. The county jail could provide neither.

Indiana State Police and the Monticello Police Department were still trying to figure out where she had obtained the revolver used in the shooting. Ballistics at the state police laboratory confirmed that it was the gun that killed Cobb and wounded his girlfriend. Except for where she had procured the gun, which was unknown, she was linked to the gun, as her fingerprints were all over it, and the farmer had seen her car in the location where the gun had been found by police.

On Thursday, February 5, a search warrant was issued for the 1971 light green Oldsmobile 98 that Lois had driven the day of the murder. The car was impounded. Police recovered the bullet that had gone through Lois's shoulder, through the seat and into the back seat. The warrant was only a formality. Police already knew it was there.

A couple of days later, Dr. Hunt sent a letter to the court to report on Lois. He said in the letter that Lois was still trembling from the experience and that she was very tense. She spoke of her sadness and hopelessness for the future. She felt dejected. Dr. Hunt asked her about her hand, and she replied, "I deserve a bad hand." She spoke of failing everyone and even failing at suicide.

Hunt further said in the letter that she seemed aware of her current situation and that she needed further psychiatric treatment. She was still severely depressed but not suicidal. He recommended continued treatment and admission to Norman Beatty Memorial Hospital.

On February 24, Dr. Iver F. Small wrote a letter to the court from the Women's State Prison saying that Lois was preoccupied with her sadness, her guilt from killing her husband and the injustices that her ex-husband had dealt her. He said she cried continuously. Her hands were always wet with perspiration of deep emotion. He said her psychotic, depressive action was complicated by drugs and alcohol.

The next day she was transferred from the prison to LaRue Carter Hospital in Indianapolis. Don Batcheldor was appointed as her guardian.

On March 4, the divorce case was dismissed for obvious reasons. It had been set for March 25.

About this time, a memorial fund was started at the State and Savings Bank in Monticello in memory of Dr. Cobb. The proceeds were supposed to be used to erect a forty-foot flagpole at the new Twin Lakes track, and a bronze plaque would be placed at this base in memory of him. The fund was stopped because of the controversy. Michael said he was asked if he minded if it went away, and he told them no, so the flagpole and plaque never came about.

Also in March, the White County Circuit Court appointed two psychiatrists—Dr. Hunt and Dr. David L. Evans—to examine Lois again and report back to the court. Dr. Hunt reported back to the court in a letter dated April 11. In that letter, he said, "Her emotional expression was one of sadness and dejection and she spoke in a very slow and meticulous manner." He also stated she was tearful at times; however, he felt that her judgment was adequate.

A month later, Dr. Evans sent a letter on May 12. He wrote, "The severe and long-standing depressive illness that she has and its effect on her ability to make her defense would be the only existing important psychiatric considerations that I would see as possibly relevant." He also stated she had trouble recalling details, but he found no psychiatric unfitness on her being charged.

Also in May, Mike graduated with a bachelor's degree from Purdue University.

On June 20, Dr. Small wrote the court that she had been given antidepressants but that she didn't respond to that treatment, so she was given shock treatment a dozen times; her mood had improved considerably. However, he noted that her memory and orientation were impaired. He didn't recommend that she go to court for another four to six weeks.

A month later, on July 15, Small wrote the court to report that she had recovered from her psychiatric treatment. She was able to understand the nature of her criminal action. "Her thought processes are reasonably normal except for some paranoid ideation and most of her depression has lifted," he wrote. She still had trouble remembering details, however.

A day later, Dr. Evans wrote the court saying that she was capable of standing trial now.

On July 22, during an arraignment on the grand jury charges, Lois's attorney, Jack Guy, filed a plea of insanity. Lois didn't want to go to trial. Prosecuting attorney John Million denied the plea.

A couple of days later, Million requested a change in judges, so the White County Circuit Court disqualified Judge Zerface and recommended three other judges for the case: Judge Harold R. Staffeldt, Pulaski Circuit Court; Judge Newell A. Lamb, Newton Circuit Court; and Judge Perry R. Shipman, Benton Circuit Court.

On the same day, the White County Circuit Court appointed three doctors to examine Lois again before the trial, set for September. Besides Dr. Small, who had already examined her, Dr. Ronald H. Hall and Dwight W. Schuster were appointed.

Two weeks later, on August 11, Judge Staffeldt was appointed as the special judge to hear the Cobb case. Million accepted the appointment.

Guy requested all the documents in the case on August 22 to get ready for the trial.

Two weeks later, on September 3, the trial date was moved from September 22 until October 21 at 9:30 a.m.

Dr. Schuster reported to the circuit court on September 4 in a letter. He stated, "I believe that as a result of mental disease that Mrs. Cobb lacked substantial capacity to conform her conduct to the requirement of the law on that date." He said that she had had an acute schizophrenic episode in September. He also said that her memory was poor about what happened around Christmastime.

Dr. Small went even further with his opinion of Lois. He stated, "In very plain, simple terms, I believe from July 1974 through July 1975, Mrs. Cobb was out of her mind." He recommended continued treatment for mental illness.

Dr. Hull disagreed. He stated, "[I]t is my opinion that her ability to appreciate the wrongfulness of her conduct or to conform her conduct to the requirement of the law were not compromised by a mental disease or defect at the time."

Jack countered with a plea of voluntary manslaughter.

Armed with the doctor's findings, Million, who is still an attorney in town, decided that it would be in the best interest of the county that he accept the plea rather than go through the trial and might end up with a not guilty by means of insanity judgment. He explained that four of five psychiatrists believed that she was insane at the time of the murder. He figured that a trial would take a couple of weeks and cost the county some $5,000, so the plea saved the county money and found her guilty of manslaughter, although the conviction wasn't exactly what the law prescribed. Voluntary manslaughter at that time meant that the person killed someone voluntarily in a sudden heat and without malice. Lois had actually plotted the murder and had malice, so the plea didn't fit the crime, but it gave a closure to the case and satisfied all parties concerned. The judge could have declined the plea if he had felt differently.

At the hearing, Judge Staffeldt asked Guy how the defendant would plead in the case.

Lois stood up and said, "Guilty!" She did so in a strong, clear voice, according to court records.

"Do you understand the charges against you?" the judge asked.

"Yes," she replied.

"Do you understand that pleading guilty that you waive all rights to a jury trial in which you might confront witnesses against you and produce witnesses?"

"Yes."

"Have you received any promises in return for pleading guilty?"

"No."

"I'm satisfied with the factual basis for the amended charge against you and accept your plea," the judge said. Judge Staffeldt scheduled the sentencing for Tuesday, October 28. He also referred the case to White County probation officer Bill Green.

At the sentencing hearing, Guy called three witnesses: Dr. Small, Reverend Helm and Don Batcheldor, guardian of Lois's two children. Small said that she had been out of her mind for a year. Helm said that her religious beliefs were deeper now. Batcheldor said that she had always been active in the community and had been a good mother and housewife. He had never seen any violent tendencies in her until her marital problems occurred.

In Guy's summation, he called the incident a "tragedy." "Four of five psychiatrists who examined her didn't feel she met the Indiana test to be tried on the charges filed, your honor," he said. "The plea bargain is in the best interests of my client. I ask for the mercy of the court in suspending her sentence. Instead, she should be required to re-admit herself to LaRue Carter Hospital."

"This is one of the most unusual cases I've ever heard," Judge Staffeldt said, according to court records. Then he accepted the plea and gave her a sentence of two to twenty years in prison but also gave her credit for time served (279 days) and suspended the rest of the prison sentence. He then gave her five years in probation and required her to readmit herself to LaRue Carter, where she would stay until doctors determined that hospitalization was no longer advisable.

Lois spent about six more months at LaRue Carter before she was released and began serving probation, according to her daughter. She was put in a halfway house in Indianapolis and began working at the Indianapolis Airport as a waitress, according to a former friend.

Then in January 1978, Marshal Green requested her probation be ended. The court agreed and her probation expired on January 9. She was a free woman again.

When Lois got out of the hospital, she went back to living like a normal person very quickly. She soon married a man by the name of Burt Ballinger. He was an alcoholic, though, and the marriage ended in divorce after a decade.

Then Lois married a man who was fourteen years older than her. He's now ninety-one years old and feeble, but she loves him and takes care of him. His name is Robert Van Orsdol, and they live in North Carolina.

Julie is still in contact with her mother, who is "extremely remorseful" over the murder of her first husband. But that chapter of her life is behind her, and she is very content with her life now.

Mike doesn't want anything to do with his mother and hasn't spoken to her since the murder of his father. He lives in east Monticello on Lake

Freeman with his wife, and they have had two daughters. He's a manager for Vanguard in Monon and has been with the company since 1981.

He and his sister see each other often, although they are miles apart. Julie ended up marrying a Middleton and lives in Fort Wayne. She is a stay-at-home mom and takes care of their five children.

Perhaps Lois's background had something to do with that fateful day when she lost it. Her mother died of tuberculosis when she was four years old. Her father didn't know how to take care of her and pawned her off on another family member he knew. "She didn't live a normal childhood," Julie said.

"She got away with murder," Mike now says, reflecting on the decision.

In any case, history can't be changed. The clock can't be turned back. Like the infamous local tornado, the case sticks in the minds of Monticello residents who lived here at the time, and they talk about it like they talk about the twister that changed the city forever.

DRUNKEN MAN KILLS GIRLFRIEND IN CRASH

A few people have lost their lives due to traffic accidents in Monticello over the past one hundred years. One of those tragedies occurred in 1998.

Constance "Connie" Wheeldon and Michael Rowlands went shopping at Kmart on Sunday, October 4, 1998. Connie had been working at a local bar, and Michael had been drinking there. After shopping, they left Kmart at 5:55 p.m. Rowlands drove behind the store. As he turned behind the Kmart, he took the corner too wide and headed into a semi-truck trailer parked behind the store.

"Look out!" Connie yelled to him.

He couldn't react quickly enough and slammed into the semi. Connie was killed instantly when her side of the 1979 Ford pickup truck rammed underneath the truck. The hood and cab were smashed in and lodged beneath the trailer, owned by Rent-A-Truck of Peru.

Rowlands ran around to the front of Kmart to call the police. He was covered with blood. Monticello police officer Curt Blount, now the city police chief, got the call to respond. When he got to the accident scene, he could hardly believe his eyes and said, "Holy shit!" on his radio. To him, it almost looked like Connie had lost her head in the accident, but there's no truth to the rumor that she was decapitated in the accident. Coroner Bernie

Michael Rowlands buried his Ford pickup truck under this semi behind the Kmart in Monticello. *Courtesy of the Monticello Police Department.*

Cook wrote that she died from contusions, hemorrhages, lacerations and bruises to both lungs.

The accident was the first fatal one that Blount had ever covered, so he called for a supervisor to help with the investigation. "There were no skid marks," said Blount in an interview. That meant that Rowlands didn't slam on the brakes before hitting the truck.

"He said he was going too fast," Blount recalled after reviewing the police report.

Blount didn't perform a breathalyzer test at the scene because of Rowlands's injuries. Rowlands was taken to the White County Hospital for treatment and was tested for alcohol there at 7:01 p.m. by Dr. Asuhail Rahhal. The result was .131 blood alcohol content, which was much higher than the law (.10) allowed back then. Meanwhile, Connie's body was taken to the Voorhis-Draper Funeral Home.

On Monday, police arrested Rowlands at 8:40 p.m. on a warrant charging him with the death of his twenty-six-year-old girlfriend.

The next day, he was arraigned in White County Superior Court. He said he couldn't afford counsel, so the court appointed Sheryl Phearson to represent him. He pleaded not guilty to the charge of operating a vehicle with an unlawful blood alcohol content causing death with a prior unrelated conviction, a Class B felony. Judge Robert B. Mrzlack gave him a bail of $50,000.

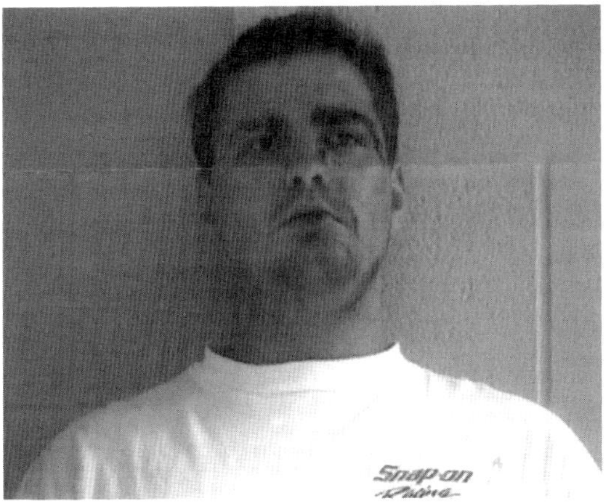

Michael Rowlands shows some marks on his face from the crash that killed his girlfriend. *Courtesy of the White County Sheriff's Department.*

This wasn't the first time Rowlands had been drinking and driving. In July that year, he pleaded guilty to operating a vehicle while intoxicated, a Class A misdemeanor, and was sentenced to one year in jail. The jail sentence was suspended, and Rowlands was placed on informal probation for one year.

On Wednesday, Connie's body was shown at the funeral home, and she was buried the next day at Buffalo Cemetery.

On November 25, the court set a pretrial for January 21 at 8:30 a.m. The trial was set for February 2. Meanwhile, Rowland sat in the White County Jail, unable to post bond. However, a motion to reduce the bond was filed by his attorney. Four days later, the court changed the bond to $10,000 cash and a property bond of $40,000. A week later, David X. Rowlands posted the bond, and Rowlands was released from White County jail on bond.

Less than one month later, he officially separated from his wife, Julie L. Rowlands. The two had married on August 9, 1992, in White County. They had two children: Shane Michael, age seven; and Jessica L., age eight.

One month later, on January 21, Rowlands worked out a plea agreement with prosecutor Robert Guy. He pleaded guilty to operating a vehicle with an unlawful blood alcohol content causing death with a prior unrelated conviction, a Class B felony The court sentenced him on February to ten years in prison and five years' probation. Instead of sending him directly to a state facility, he was sent to White County jail again, which didn't sit too well with Rowlands.

His former boss, Stephen Price, sent a letter to the court. "I would like greatly to see that he be able to continue to help financially support them [his children] by working here at Beck Muffler on a work release program." The letter had no influence on the court, and Rowlands could do nothing but sit in jail.

On May 11, 1999, Rowlands sent a letter to Judge Mrzlack requesting to be transferred to a Department of Corrections facility.

On June 11, 1999, his wife filed for divorce.

Then on July 11, 1999, Rowlands sent a letter to Judge Mrzlack asking to be put on a work crew. The judge responded two days letter, saying that he had no jurisdiction to do either that or transfer him to another department facility.

On December 28, 1999, Rowlands's new attorney, Brian G. Dekker, filed a motion to modify the sentence. Judge Mrzlack denied the motion on January 1, 2000. Dekker filed a motion to reconsider, and Mrzlack denied that, too.

The divorce to his wife was finalized on March 28, 2000.

On July 5, 2002, Rowlands again asked for placement in a Department of Corrections facility but this time for the substance abuse program. Judge Mrzlack took his time denying that request one year later.

Rowlands was released on good behavior on October 20, 2003, and went on probation for five years.

He went back to working at Beck Muffler, so his wife filed for child support in May 2004 and started receiving support of fifty dollars per week from her ex-husband. She also changed her last name to "Poppy."

Rowlands's probation ended on October 24, 2008.

PART III

CARROLL COUNTY

SUSPECT HANGED BY LYNCH MOB

The Wabash River has been the site of several deaths over the years because of accidents, floods and even one murder way back in 1887.

On a Sunday morning, a farmer and his son were taking a stroll along the Wabash River about nine miles southwest of Lafayette when they came across a body in the ice and slush. The naked body was so badly decomposed that they couldn't tell if it was that of a man or woman. The men hurried back to their farmhouse and then sent a message to notify the coroner.

Deputy Coroner J.K. Hill and an undertaker from Lancaster & Connell drove down to the scene of the terrible discovery. Hill used a pick and spade to get the body out of the icy river. They put the body in a plain wooden coffin and hauled it back to Lafayette for further examination.

The coroner estimated that the body had been in the river for several months. He decided that the body was that of a woman who had a front tooth broken off and a decayed one next to it. The coroner was not aware that police were looking for a woman, Luella Mabbitt. The twenty-three-year-old blonde woman had been missing since August 3.

A couple of days later, the parents of the missing woman—William Mabbitt and his wife, Ella—were asked to come to the funeral home to view the remains and identify them. William viewed the remains first and thought that they were of his daughter. Mrs. Mabbitt then viewed them and nearly fainted.

An autopsy was performed on the body by two doctors, who decided that she had died from drowning.

Authorities quickly found out that her life had been threatened by Amer C. Green, so a warrant was put out for his arrest by the Tippecanoe prosecuting attorney. Sheriffs in Carroll, Cass and Tippecanoe Counties were asked to help capture Green.

Green lived in Young America, which was located in southern Cass County. Sheriff J.B. "Buck" Stanley went there to discover if Green was there. He wasn't. During the investigation, he found a trunk belonging to Amer's brother, Bill. In the trunk, he found a twenty-six-dollar railroad fare to Sherman. He didn't know where that was, but he checked with railroad officials and found that a fare to Sherman, Texas, was indeed twenty-six dollars. That clue of his whereabouts led Green to go to Texas to hunt down the brothers, as Bill Green was also wanted for murder.

The sheriff left in mid-June and started his search in Granville, Texas. He hooked up with a county sheriff there who helped him in his hunt. At a town named Kentucky, the postmaster recalled a man who fit the description of Amer and had a hunchback, except the man was using the name of Frank Hartsman and his brother was known as Charlie Hartsman. These men had gone off to Tascosa, New Mexico, so Sheriff Stanley went there. The city marshal and sheriff there knew the Hartsman brothers, and they had just gone in different directions to work. Sheriff Stanley went after Bill and sent another sheriff to capture Amer. Stanley was successful and hauled Bill back to Tascosa. When he got there, the other sheriff already had Amer in jail. After Sheriff Wallace shackled Amer, he tried to crawl over to a Winchester rifle, but Wallace stopped him a few feet short of the gun.

Before Sheriff Stanley returned to Logansport, word spread around the city that the Greens had been caught and were returning to jail there. Soon after their arrival, more than 1,000 persons gathered around the jail, including William Mabbitt. A rumor went around that 150 men on horseback from the Young America community south of the city were coming to hang the men, so the sheriff had to hire 22 additional men to guard the jail. Even Judge Winfield was on hand with his Winchester rifle to keep the peace. The crowd was kept fifty feet from the jail. To give them more protection before trial, the Greens were sent to the state prison in Michigan City. Bill Green was later tried in Peru and given a life sentence for killing Enos Brumbaugh. Amer Green's trial was moved to the Carroll County Circuit Court to give him a fair trial.

On October 21, 1887, Amer was arraigned before the circuit court, but the indictment was faulty and the prosecutor had to void it. A motion was sustained, and a special session of the grand jury was called immediately to return a new indictment.

Meanwhile, Amer was put in the Delphi jail. Some 250 men gathered and rode into Delphi that night. Sheriff Van Gundy stood ready to protect his prisoner, but he was easily overpowered. He refused to surrender the keys to the jail, so the masked men battered the door with sledgehammers and knocked it from its hinges. The mob then got through the three remaining heavy iron doors to Amer.

He was put on a horse, and the men took him toward Flora about 1:00 a.m. He was taken to the vicinity of the Mabbitt home, which was near Walnut Grove. Friends of the Mabbitts had erected large bonfires to guide the mob to the site.

They asked him to confess, but he refused, so they tortured him in various ways. He claimed that she was still alive. "I would have produced Luella Mabbitt on the day of my trial," he told the angry mob, according to the *Lafayette Daily Journal*.

When it became obvious to them that he wasn't going to confess, the mob decided to kill him. Some wanted to burn him, while the majority said to hang him. The last words of the thirty-five-year-old were: "Inform my mother, send her my body, and tell her I desire to be buried next to my sister in Ohio."

They left him there to hang in the gloom of the night for a while and then cut him down about 2:00 a.m. They took his body to Flora.

PART IV

WARREN COUNTY

WOMAN CUTS UP VICTIMS, STUFFS IN SUITCASES

Due south of Lafayette is the little town of Darlington in Warren County. The town of fewer than a thousand people has a covered bridge, but it is more well known as the birthplace of Winnie Ruth Judd, one of America's crime legends.

This daughter of a minister, Reverend Harvey McKinnell, grew up in Darlington in the Roaring Twenties, but after she grew up she headed west and ended up in Phoenix, Arizona, where she married Dr. William Craig Judd and worked as a medical secretary for him.

On October 16, 1931, the attractive blue-eyed blonde planned to spend the weekend with her closest friend, Hedvig "Sammy" Samuelson, and her roommate, Agnes Anne LeRoi. That night, she waited until they were asleep before she shot them to death.

The next morning, Winnie went to work with her left hand bandaged.

She later cut up the bodies and stuffed them into two train trunks. She put them onto a train headed to Los Angeles on October 19. The baggage handler became suspicious of the trunks because of the foul smell coming from both and the brownish liquid coming from one of them. They were set aside for inspection. When Winnie's brother, Burton J. McKinnell, went to claim her trunks, officials told him that they would have to be opened before they could give them to him, so he walked away.

When police opened the trunks, they found the bodies. One had been crammed into a jackknife position. The second trunk contained the dismembered parts of another woman. Both had been shot in the head. Another suitcase found abandoned in a restroom contained a torso.

Police detectives found Winnie's ailing husband in the city. He was surprised to hear that she was in town.

Winnie finally called her husband on October 23, as well as their attorney. She told police that her friend Sammy had shot her in the hand. When the bullet was removed, doctors saw that her body was bruised.

A plumber found a torn-up letter written by Winnie in the drainpipe of a Los Angeles department store and turned it over to police. She had spent a night in the store hiding from the police. The letter was addressed to her husband and confessed to the crimes. She explained in the letter that Sammy had shot her in the hand and that she had retaliated by shooting her. Then she shot Anne to prevent her from blackmailing her. She claimed self-defense.

Winnie then changed her tune and accused her victims of being "perverts," but the facts of the case disputed that claim.

She was taken to trial in 1932, and her defense team tried to paint her as insane to avoid a death sentence. An all-male jury saw otherwise and found her guilty of first-degree murder.

Her attorneys appealed the case but lost, so she tried another angle. She went to a grand jury to tell them that she was involved with another man, who helped her stuff the bodies into the trunks. The grand jury indicted the man and asked the parole board to commute her sentence to life. The board didn't agree, so Judd's attorney asked for a sanity hearing. With three days left before the hanging, Winnie put on a show of crying and screaming at the hearing that convinced the jury to send her to a mental hospital instead of the gallows.

The man indicted by the grand jury never went to trial, as officials saw through her strategy.

She was sent to the Arizona State Hospital for the Insane in Phoenix in 1933. After six years in the institution, she began escaping from it. She broke out twice in 1939 for six days the first time and twelve the next. When she asked to attend the funeral of her husband in 1945, she was denied. She got out for twelve hours in 1951 and for thirteen hours twice in 1952.

The asylum superintendent had said that Winnie Ruth had agreed not to escape anymore. Six months later, she broke out again. According to the truTV website, when she was captured, she told them, "Why don't you leave me alone? I'm so tired of being locked up. They say I'm dangerous. I'm not."

She escaped the hospital again in 1962 and left the state to work as a maid in California. To hide her identity, she changed her name to Marian Lane. However, she was fingerprinted during a murder investigation in Danville, California, in June 1969, and officers uncovered her true identity—the famed "Tiger Woman" of the 1930s. However, she was not connected to the murder. She was sent back to Arizona again.

In December 1971, the Arizona Parole Board released her just before Christmas. She moved back to Danville, California, and assumed the name of Marian Lane again to hide her true identity. Now in her late sixties, she was caring for a garden and an assortment of animals, including a tomcat and an eel.

She died at age ninety-three on October 23, 1998. She will long be remembered as the "trunk murderess."

PART V

BENTON COUNTY

MAN KILLS BRIDE TO BE

One of the most recent murders involving people from Tippecanoe County occurred during the writing of this book. The day after Thanksgiving in 2009, a Lafayette man was accused of killing a forty-year-old West Lafayette woman in rural Benton County. Steven R. Farrell fatally shot his fiancée, Christine R. Craig, on the day they were to be married.

Christine was driving her vehicle on a county road in Benton County when she pulled up next to Steven, who was driving his pickup. Riding with him was Christine's sixteen-year-old daughter, Jazlyn Travnicek. She got out of Farrell's truck and spoke with her mother. Christine then confronted Steven. Afterward, she walked back around her car and entered the passenger side of the vehicle. Jazlyn jumped into the driver's side of the car. That's when Steven walked over to the passenger's side of the car and shot Christine in the chest. Farrell then returned to his own pickup and left the scene. Jazlyn drove her mother to the Fellure's Foods in Otterbein, where she died from her injuries before medical personnel arrived.

The fifty-seven-year-old Farrell was captured on video surveillance later that day at the Indianapolis International Airport. A national search was conducted for the suspect while the Benton Circuit Court charged him with murder. The suspect was spotted in Utah one week later and then captured in

The Mesquite Police Department in Nevada took Steven R. Farrell into custody and photographed him when he was booked into jail there. He was then transferred to the Las Vegas Police Department for holding until he could be sent back to Indiana for trial. *Courtesy of the Mesquite Police Department.*

Nevada on December 9. He was staying at the Valley Inn Motel in Mesquite when authorities took him into custody.

Farrell is expected to be tried in 2010 in Benton County, according to prosecuting attorney Bill Weist. Farrell fought his extradition to Indiana. "We anticipated that he would refuse extradition," Weist said, according to a *Lafayette Journal & Courier* article. His extradition finally occurred at the end of January.

Weist is not seeking the death penalty in the case. The last murder to go to trial in the county was held in 1998.

Bibliography

Clark County Prosecuting Attorney's Office. Indiana Death Row. "James Lowery." http://www.clarkprosecutor.org/html/death/row/loweryj.htm.

———. "Joseph L. Trueblood." http://www.clarkprosecutor.org/html/death/US/trueblood858.htm.

Geringer, Joseph. "Winnie Ruth Judd: 'The Trunk Murderess' in Perspective." http://www.trutv.com/library/crime/notorious_murders/women/judd/3.html.

The Indiana Law Blog. "Unsolved Tippecanoe County Courthouse Bombing Nearly Ten Years Old." http://www.indianalawblog.com/archives/2008/05/ind_courts_unso.html.

"Ku Klux Klan." Wikipedia, the free encyclopedia. http://en.wikipedia.org/wiki/Ku_Klux_Klan.

Lafayette, Indiana Police Department. http://lafayette.in.gov/police.

NewspaperARCHIVE.com. http://www.newspaperarchive.com.

"Temperance Movement." Wikipedia, the free encyclopedia. http://en.wikipedia.org/wiki/Temperance_movement.

Tippecanoe County, Indiana Sheriff's Department. http://www.tippecanoe.in.gov/sheriff.

"White Mule." Wikipedia, the free encyclopedia. http://en.wikipedia.org/wiki/White_mule.

WLFI.com. "Charges Filed in 1980 Cold Case." http://www.wlfi.com/dpp/news/local/local_wlfi_lafayette_charges_filed_in_1980_cold_case_200908271530_1.

NEWSPAPERS

Indianapolis Star News.

Lafayette Daily Courier.

Lafayette Daily Journal.

Lafayette Journal & Courier.

Lafayette Morning Journal.

Lafayette Weekly Journal.

Monticello Herald Journal.

Tippecanoe County Democrat.

ABOUT THE AUTHOR

Author W.C. "Bill" Madden has written more than twenty-five books for several publishers about automotive history, baseball history and local history. This is his second book with The History Press. He wrote *Haunted Lafayette* in 2009. He has also authored more than one hundred articles for such magazines as *Entrepreneur*.

The Monticello, Indiana resident began his journalism career in 1976 with the United States Air Force; he was an editor, photographer and journalism instructor. After finishing a twenty-year career in the military, he completed a journalism degree with Our Lady of the Lake University, San Antonio, Texas. He worked for three years for Topics Newspapers before becoming a technical writer for two different companies. Madden now works for the U.S. Census Bureau in public relations. When he retires in July 2010, he will devote himself full time to writing books. His goal is one hundred titles.

He is the vice-president of the Monticello Kiwanis and writes its newsletter. He heads the literacy committee for the Monticello Rotary and writes its newsletter, too. He's also a lifetime member of the White County Historical Society and serves on the board of directors for the Literacy Volunteers of White County. He loves to golf in his off time.